NadaDada Motel-Reno, Nevada
Coloring Book

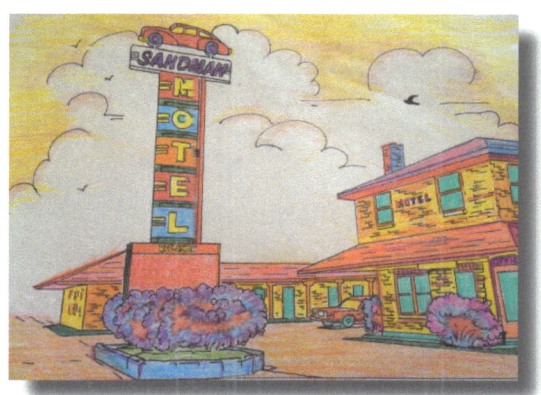

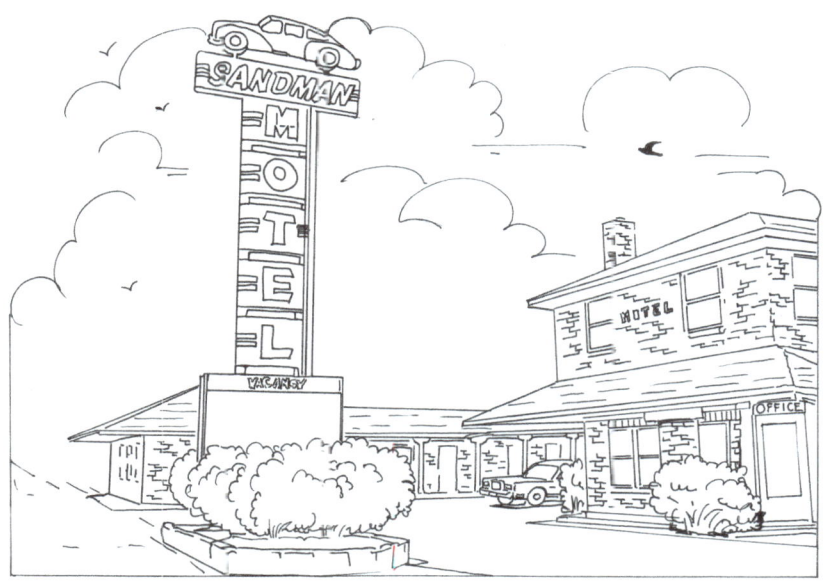

Patty Atcheson Melton

Reno Motel History Foreward
Cindy Ainsworth

The Magic of Neon
WILL Durham

NadaDada Motel-Reno, Nevada
Coloring Book

Fix Bay Inc Publishing

Patty Atcheon Melton
Foreward: Cindy Ainsworth
The Magic of Neon: Will Durham

Melton, Patty Atcheson

1. Art 2. History

ISBN: 978-0-9838149-1-7

Contents

Reno Motel History Foreward

By Cindy Ainsworth

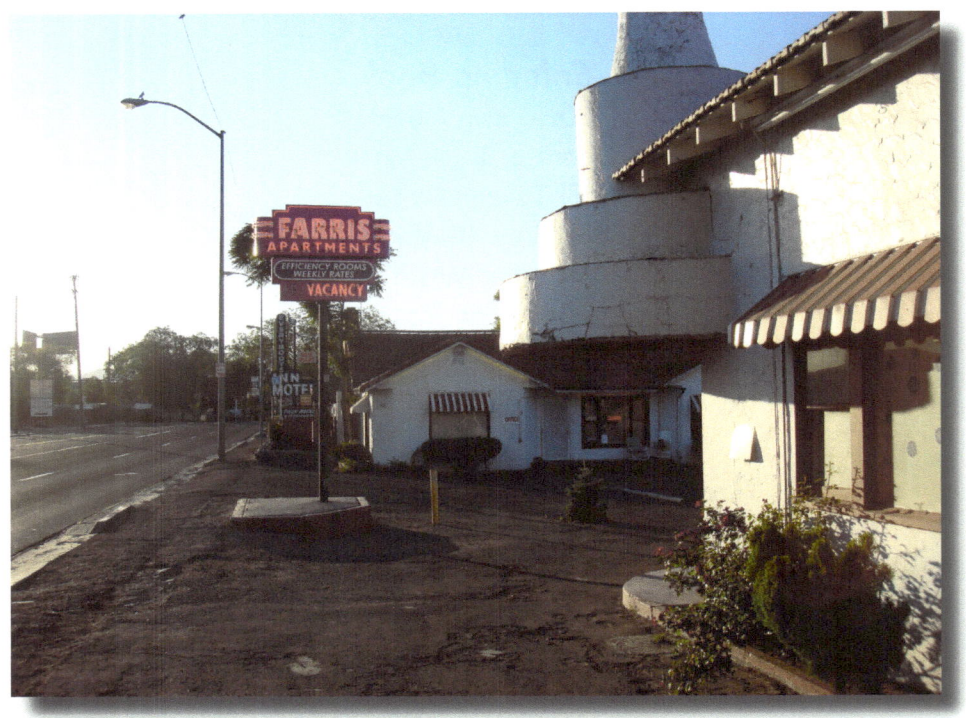

Truckee Meadows' Roadside Heritage

Why do Americans love to write about or collect items associated with our roadside culture? There's always the obvious nostalgia factor. Many recall a simpler time with no worries, traveling the back roads or highways with their families, stopping at those landmark oddities and staying at themed motels with names like Wigwam Village or the Blue Swallow. We try to recapture our childhood by collecting postcards, knickknacks or neon-trimmed clocks associated with those never-ending summer road trips. There's just something fascinating about the freedom of the open road and all that is associated with it.

While we may enjoy those car-culture items and memories, there's the serious matter of recognizing the importance of our often neglected and forgotten Truckee Meadows' roadside heritage. Reno and Sparks are lucky to still be the home to some excellent examples of motels, coffee shops and signs that reflect this mid-twentieth century commercial architectural style.

The Society of Commercial Archeology (SCA), an organization that recognizes the importance of studying, preserving and celebrating the "buildings, artifacts, structures, signs, and symbols of the twentieth century commercial landscape" stated that Reno possesses one of America's most outstanding collections of roadside architecture. "Reno's vintage motels and neon signs are a priceless part of our national heritage," announced past SCA president Michael Bedeau.

The area's roadside heritage began long before the development of the automobile. The Truckee Meadows has always had a close connection with the people who came here through the years by various modes of transportation. There were the pioneers moving on to California who traveled by wagon, horse and foot along the various emigrant and stage trails. These were the hardy individuals and families who wanted to start a new life in America's west.

The Truckee Meadows also benefited from those who stayed and worked the mines. With the discovery of the Comstock Lode gold and silver in 1859 came a need for supplies for the mining towns of Virginia City, Gold Hill and Silver City. The town site (not yet called Reno) became an important agricultural center and transportation hub with wagon freight deliveries of people and goods to and from the Comstock.

Then came the area's most important transportation development--the transcontinental railroad. The Central Pacific Railroad was pushing eastward over Donner Pass in the late 1860s. In the meantime, the enterprising Myron Lake was wheeling and dealing with Central Pacific Railroad co-founder Charles Crocker. Lake was already an important but controversial figure. In 1861, he purchased from Charles William Fuller a bridge across the Truckee River and a makeshift hotel. Lake operated the lucrative toll bridge and road much to the dissatisfaction of local citizens.

Lake would donate 160 acres to the Central Pacific in exchange to locating the depot, yards and town site north of his toll bridge. Those acres were divided into lots and auctioned on May 9, 1868, which we recognize as Reno's birthday. The town was named after Civil War general Jesse Reno. The first passenger train reached Reno in June 1868 and things would never be the same in the Truckee Meadows.

In 1872, the Virginia and Truckee Railroad would link the area with Carson City and the Comstock while the 1880 groundbreaking of the Nevada-California-Oregon Railroad would eventually connect people, cattle, sheep and lumber from the northern regions to the transcontinental railway terminus. Meanwhile, the city of Sparks was established when the Southern Pacific Railroad moved its shops there in 1904 from Wadsworth, Nevada.

Changes were on the Silver State's horizon with the development of the automobile. By 1910, there were some 450,000 registered vehicles in the United States. However, the automobilists, as they called themselves, never really thought about traveling cross-country because of the deplorable conditions of what roads existed, coupled with the additional problems of a lack of supplies and assistance for the motorists. Enter in 1913 businessman Carl Fisher, who started a campaign to establish America's first coast-to-coast highway in time for the 1915 Panama-Pacific International Exposition in San Francisco.

With private, public and commercial sponsorship assistance, Fisher's dream took hold and in 1913 the Lincoln Highway Association was incorporated. The highway name was chosen in tribute to Abraham Lincoln. The first task was to establish the route. The Association looked at maps, tested first-hand road conditions, and studied the distance between cities. Finally, the organization pieced together a 3,389-mile route from Times Square in New York City to Lincoln Park in San Francisco. The route was officially dedicated on October 31, 1913. Enthusiasm across the nation and in

Nevada was so great, that within months the route had been marked with the official Lincoln Highway signs.

Improved roads along the route were still a rarity so the second goal of the Association became the promotion of the importance of building America's highway system. Newspapers along the route, including those in Nevada, helped promote this "Good Roads Movement."

Reno was fortunate to be selected as one of the cities on the new Lincoln Highway route. From Utah, the Nevada route followed roughly what is today's Highway 50 and then onto Fallon and continuing as Highway 40 into Sparks and down Reno's East and West Fourth Street. From there, the Lincoln Highway traveler could continue south on Virginia Street to Carson City and then up over Kings Canyon Road and on to scenic Lake Tahoe. Or they could decide to continue west to Verdi and Dog Valley Road and on to Sacramento.

Locally, interest in auto travel increased tremendously as reflected in historic weekly "Reno Evening Gazette" Saturday pages devoted to road reports, auto racing and car reviews. The paper predicted in 1913 that an increase in business would be "not less than $1,000,000 in Reno the first year the roadway is open … and will bring a large increase in this dollar harvest for Reno hotels, garages, stores and restaurants." The advance of auto-related businesses not only changed the appearance of the Truckee Meadows but also contributed to the economic development of the area.

Auto camping became a popular part of recreational travel. As early as 1919, Deer Park served as Sparks' free municipal camp for auto tourists, providing a nice shady location and cool well water. These municipal camps were a common sight during the 1920s as towns nationwide catered to the automobile tourists.

The popularity of long distance travel helped in the creation of other American transcontinental roads, including the Victory Highway, which closely followed by what ia now I-80 across Nevada and East and West Fourth Street within the Reno city limits. The public's enthusiasm about improving our roads led to the involvement of the federal government, which provided Nevada with funding from the Federal-Aid Road Act. By the mid-1920s the Federal Highway System was approved and the wonderful named roads were replaced by numbered routes. By 1926, the Victory route became Highway 40 and The Lincoln route, Highway 50.

In celebration of the completion of the Lincoln and Victory Highways, the Nevada Transcontinental Highway Exposition was held throughout the summer of 1927 in Idlewild Park. During this period, Reno saw an increase in both high-end and inexpensive accommodations including the Riverside Hotel downtown and Chism's Auto Camp, which was conveniently located across the Truckee River from the Exposition.

You cannot speak about the Exposition without mentioning one of the area's most iconic landmarks. The popular Reno arch was installed in 1926 across Virginia Street at Commercial Row to promote the Exposition. To recognize the importance of automobile tourism, the 1928 Reno City Council decided the town needed a permanent slogan for the arch. A contest was held and in 1929, the slogan "Reno: Biggest Little City in the World" was installed on the arch. Today, that arch stands guard on Lake Street by the entrance of the William F. Harrah National Automobile Museum

The owners of camps and cabins realized that travelers also wanted the creature comforts of home so the auto court was born. Amenities included private baths, kitchenettes and some even provided their own cafes and gas stations. Polk's Reno City Directories listed many of these popular auto courts including the Sunset, Shady Grove (current location of the Farris Motel), Coney Island, Cremer's (location of the Pony Express Motel) and the Star.

Local factors played a significant role in establishing the need for accommodations across the region. To help survive the economic effects of the Great Depression, the 1931 Nevada legislature passed bills to legalize gaming and reduce the divorce residency requirement to six weeks. Both brought visitors to the area who filled the many hotels and auto courts in Reno and Sparks. One favorite divorce trade location was the now-gone 1927 Silver State Lodge located on West Fourth Street on the Lincoln Highway, which, according to historian Mella Harmon, "offered rustic, yet comfortable (and discreet) housing for Reno's temporary residents."

The Truckee Meadows' roadside construction really took off after World War II. Although gaming served as the region's economic giant, visitors were anxious to explore the area's natural beauty. Reno's automobile tourism boomed resulting in a proliferation of diners, gas stations and a new roadside architectural phenomenon called the motel.

A San Luis Obispo California proprietor in 1925 came up with the term motel with the establishment of the Milestone Mo-tel located halfway between Los Angeles and San Francisco. Most motel layouts usually consisted of a low-rise L or U-shaped configuration that, compared to the footprint of a high-rise hotel, required quite a bit of property. No problem since most of the motels were located on America's expansive highways. Sometimes a unique design would emerge as in the building of Reno's 1951 Sutro Motel which consists of mirror image units on the east and west sides of the street.

Reno's motel and roadside architectural renaissance continued throughout

the 1950s and into the 1960s. Motels and coffee shops were completed in anticipation of the 1960 Winter Olympics in Squaw Valley and the soon-to-be-built U.S. Highway 80. Some fine neon signs from this period still exist and include the Thunderbird Motel, Heart-O-Town, City Center Motel, the Lucky Motel, Sands Motor Inn, 7-11 Motor Lodge, Rancho Sierra and the Mid-Town Motel and Lounge, which sports one of Reno's best cocktail-glass signs.

One special motel has even been recognized by the national media. The 1949 Sandman Motel and neon sign, located at 1755 East Fourth Street, was featured in 2002 in a "USA Today" article entitled "10 Great Places to Stop Along the Way." The article described the Sandman's sign as "one of the most beautiful motel signs ever made."

The Reno and Sparks landscape changed tremendously with the completion of I-80 in 1974. The Lincoln and Victory Highways were replaced with multi-lane freeways and visitors often bypassed the historic roadways and vintage motels to stay at new high-rise resort casinos. Many of our classic motels are now weekly or monthly rentals and most are showing their age. Some people today label many of these old structures as "seedy."

But all is not lost. There is a new renaissance happening in Reno and Sparks with a fresh appreciation for our unique history and buildings. Many of our older buildings located in the Midtown section and East Fourth Street corridor are being adaptively reused for new and innovative businesses and restaurants. Our neon heritage is being preserved by Will Durham and many local pieces from his collection were displayed in an exhibit at the Nevada Museum of Art. The renegade art event NadaDada features many of our vintage motels, and the Wildflower Village's complex of motels is home to artists and galleries. This synergy keeps growing and can only contribute in the recognition and preservation of our roadside heritage.

Patty's appreciation for our wonderful motels and neon signs is reflected in this special collection of drawings. I'd like to thank her for giving us all the opportunity to have some fun while learning about our "colorful" past.

Happy Coloring!

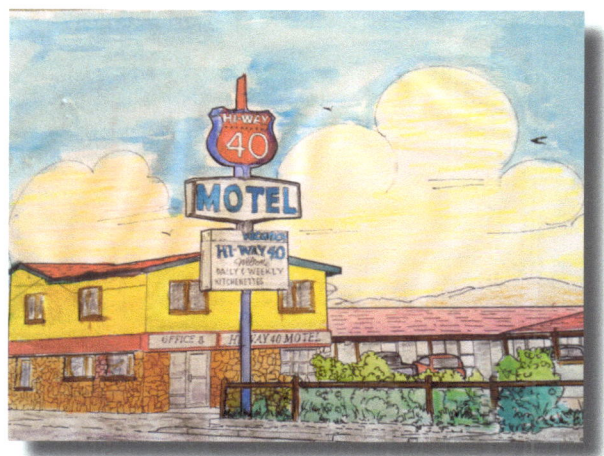

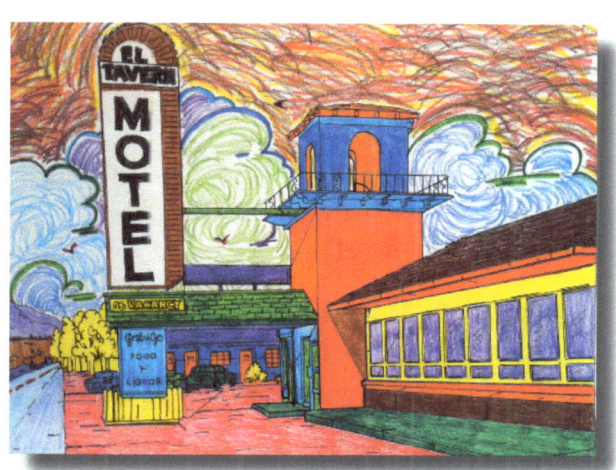

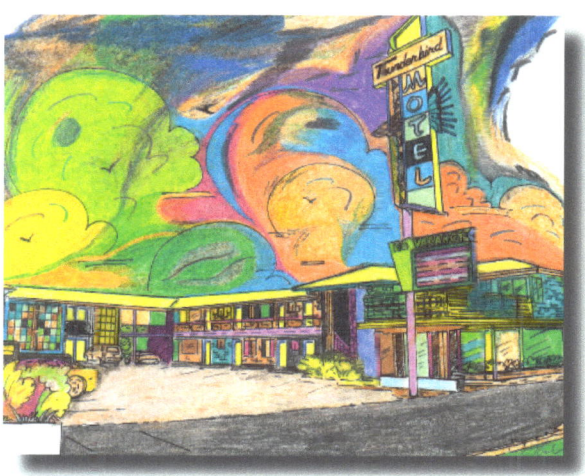

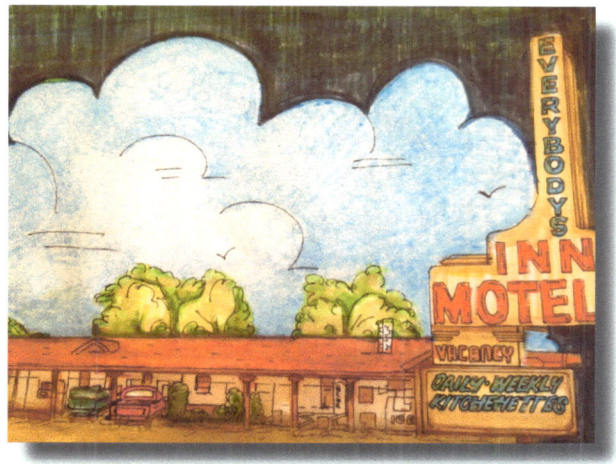

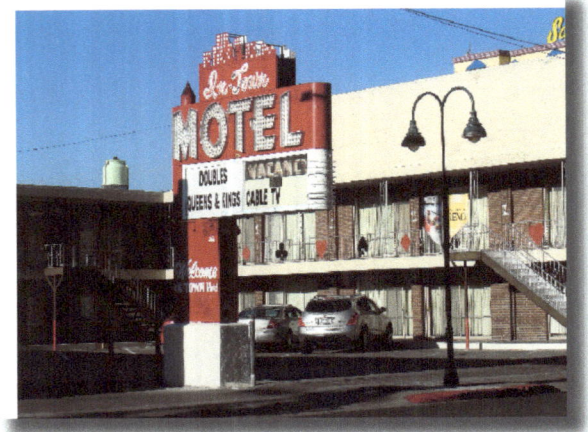

In-Town Motel

In-Town Motel's architectural design is circa 1959.

This property is at
260 W. Fourth St., Reno

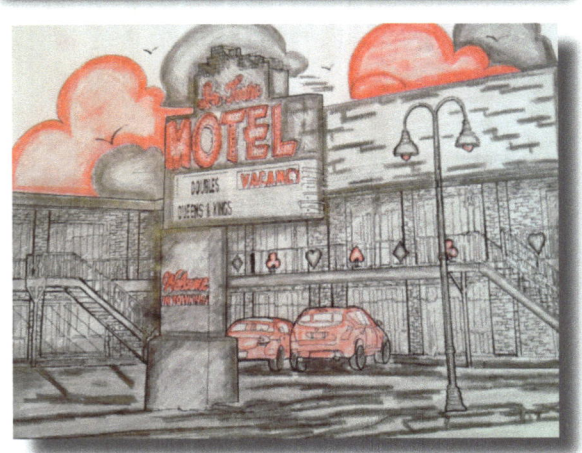

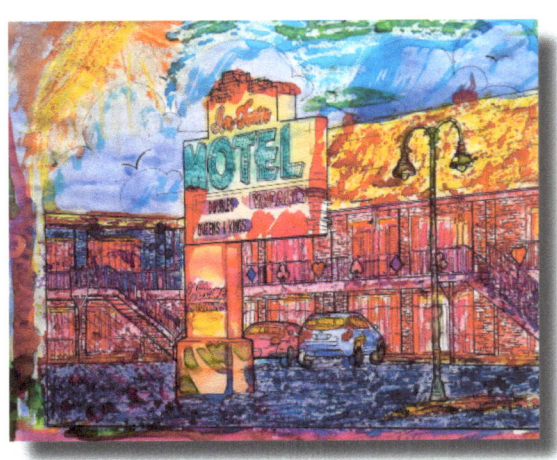

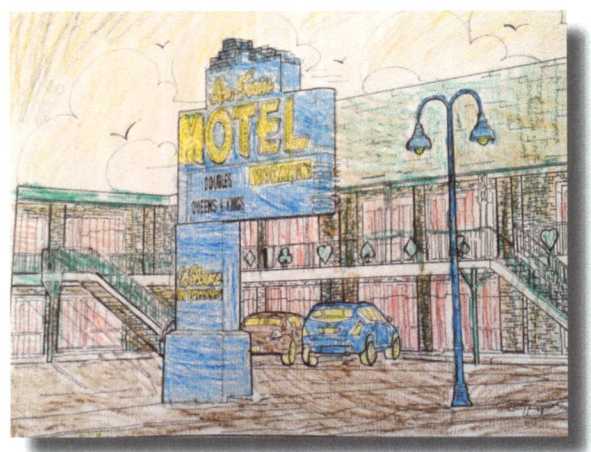

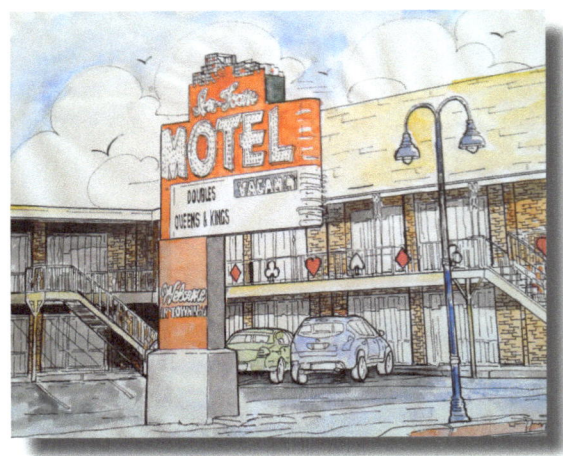

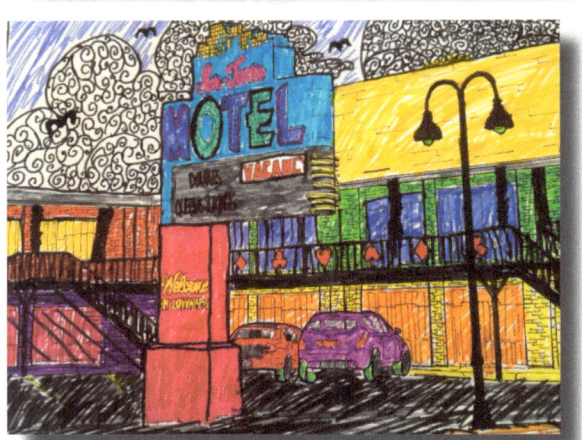

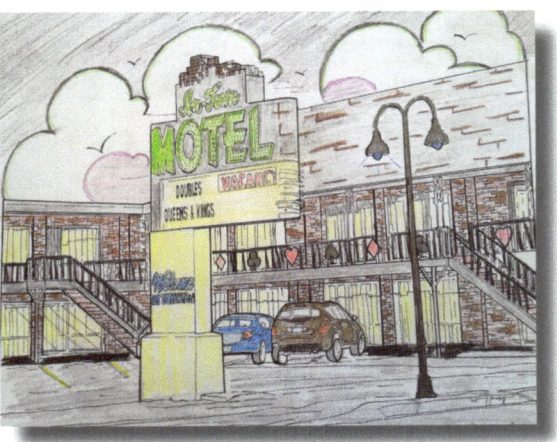

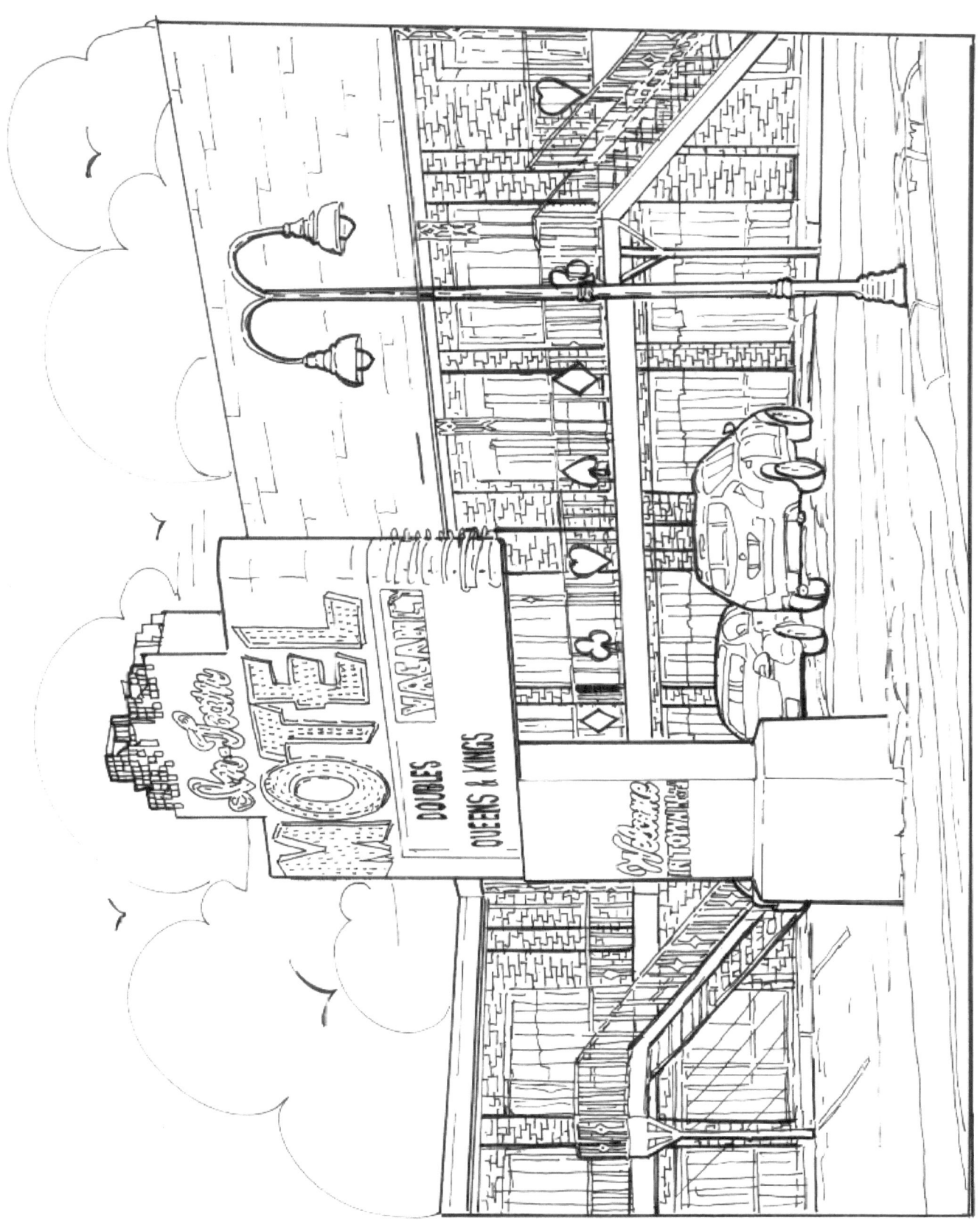

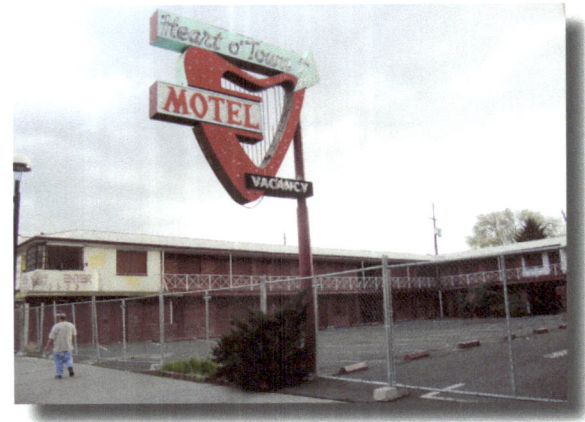

Heart o' Town

Heart o' Town Motel's
architectural design is circa 1959.

This property is at
520 N. Virginia St., Reno

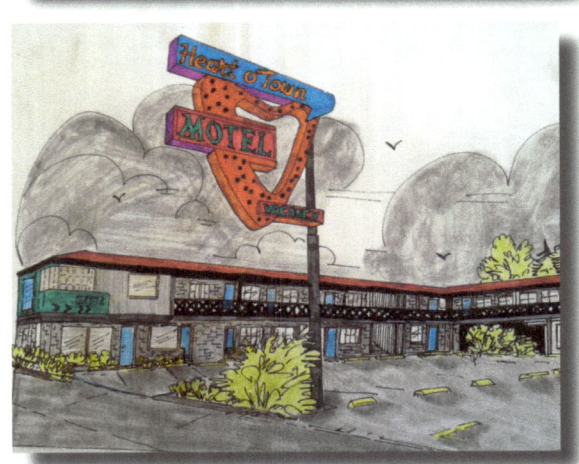

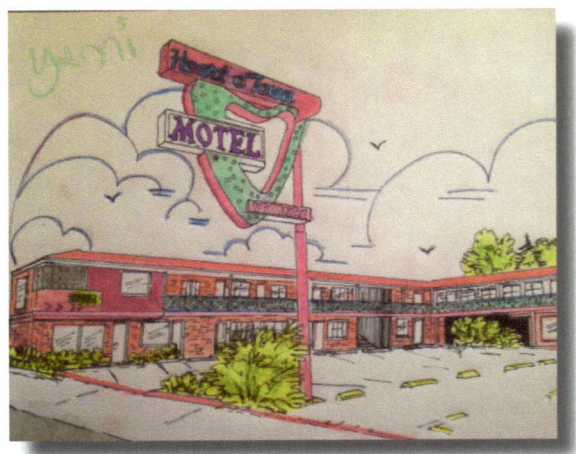

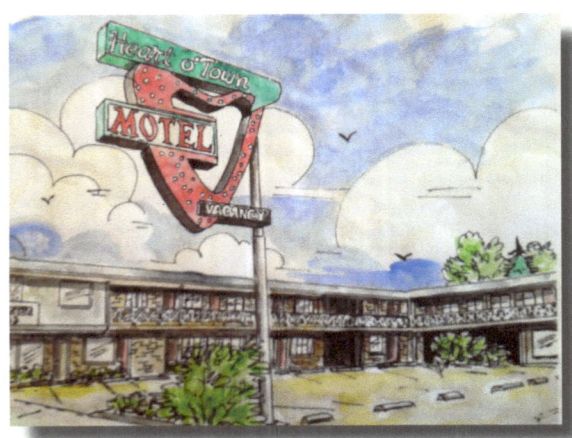

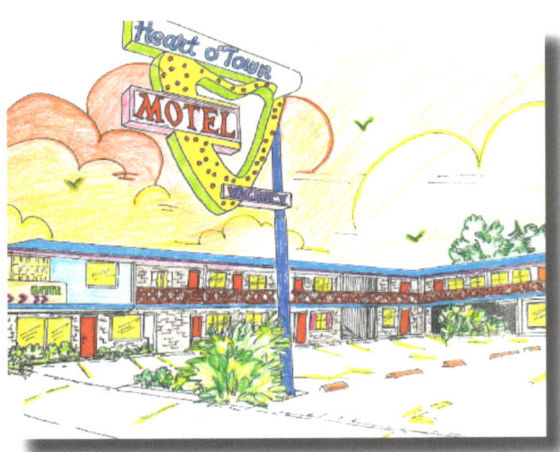

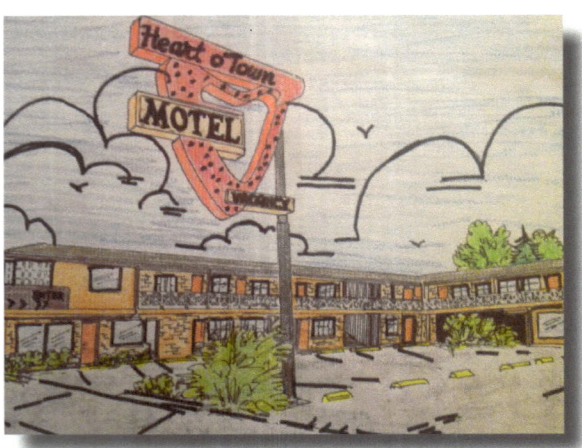

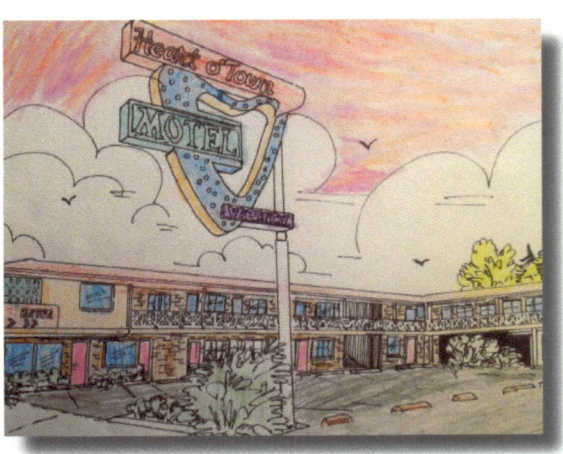

12

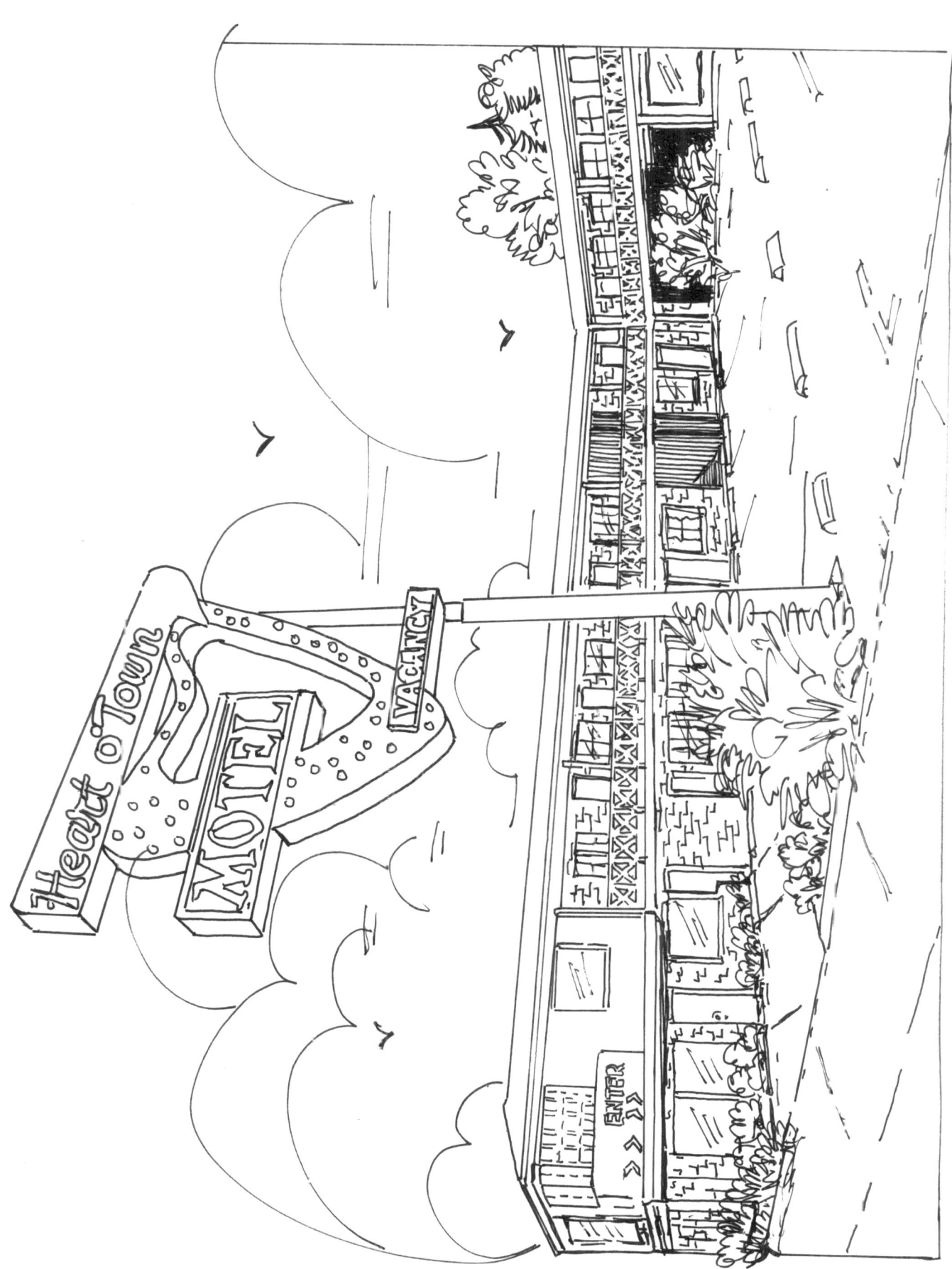

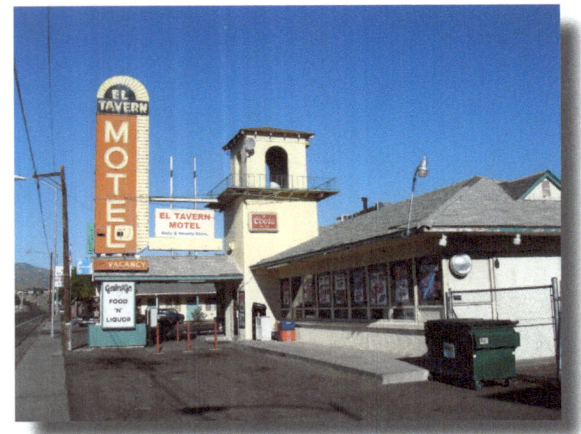

El Tavern Motel

The El Tavern Motel
was originally a nightclub
and restaurant
until it burned in 1942.
It was then rebuilt
as an auto court.

This property is at
1801 W. Fourth St., Reno

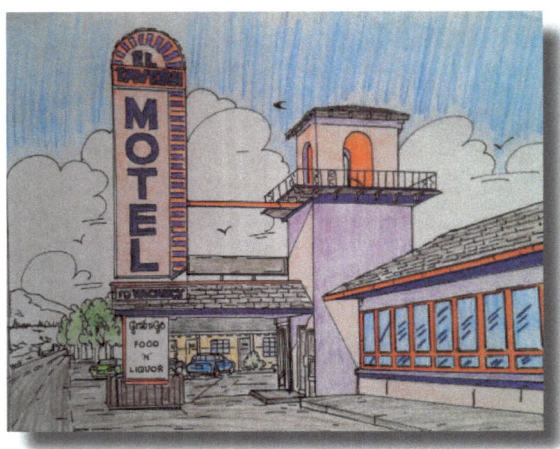

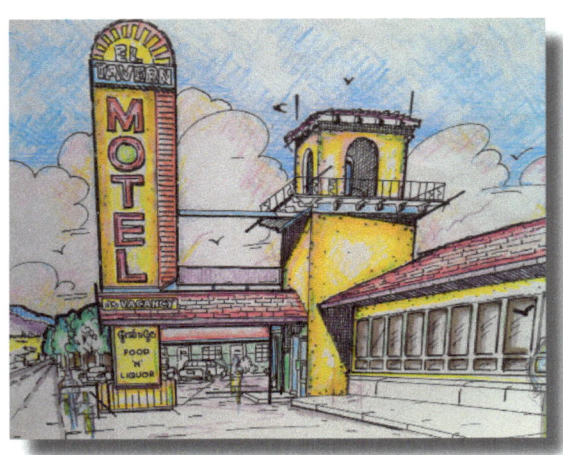

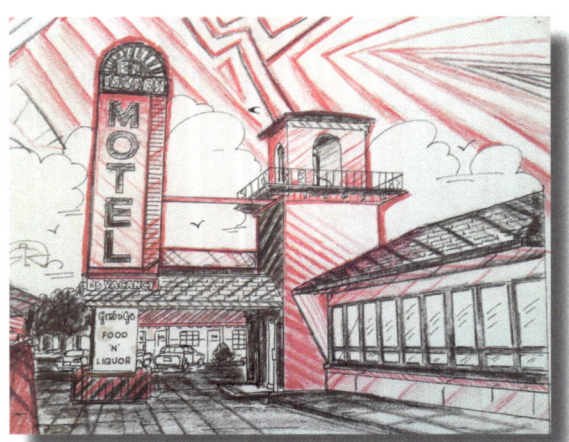

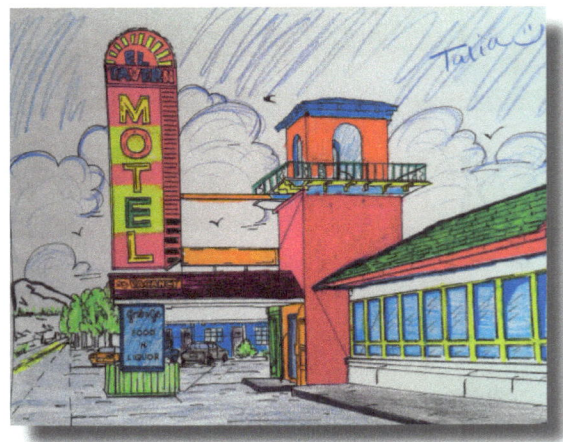

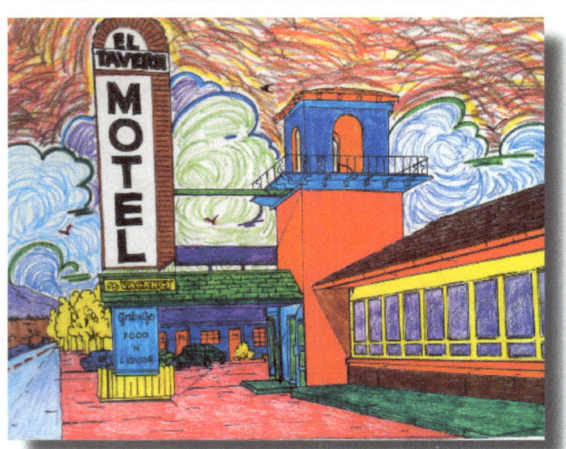

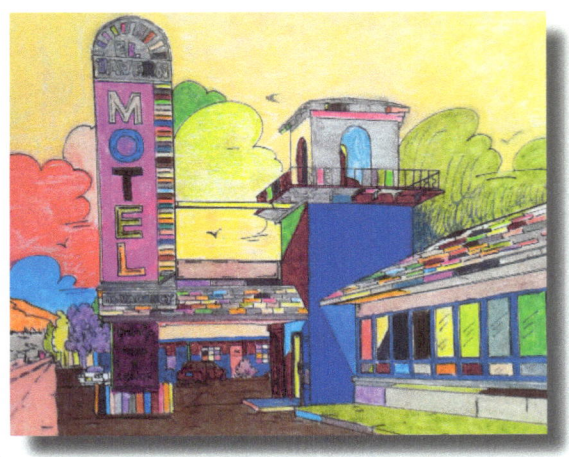

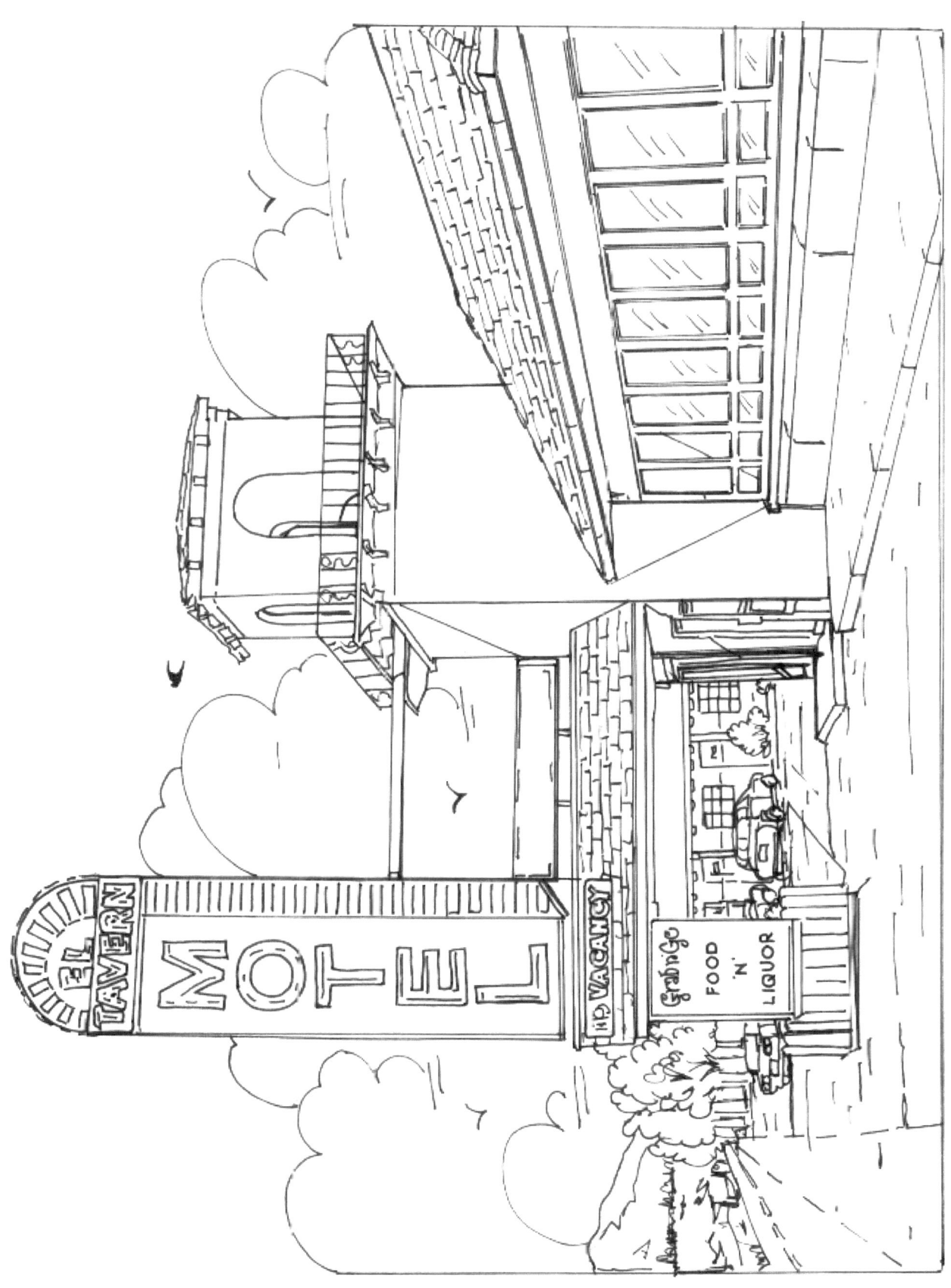

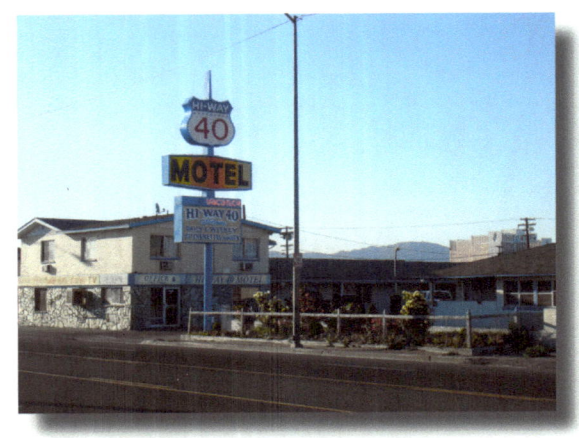

Hi Way 40 Motel

Hi Way 40 Motel's architectural design is circa 1949.

This property is at
1750 E. Fourth St., Reno

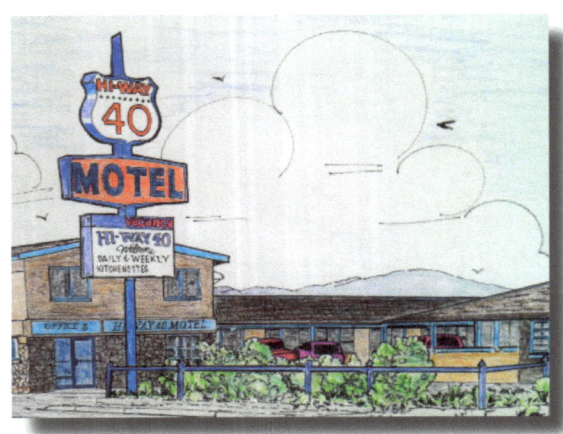

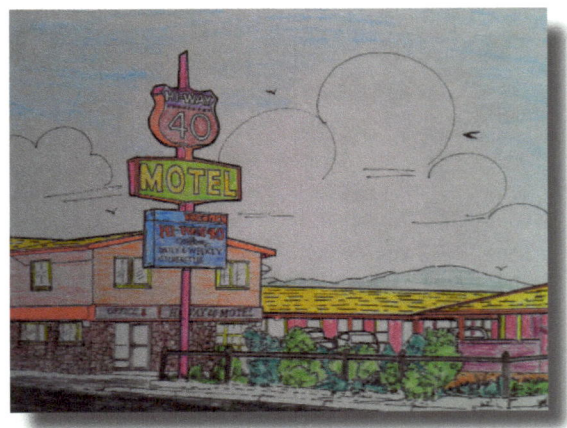

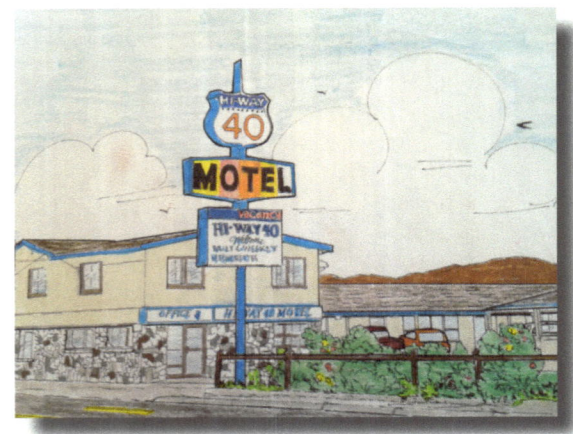

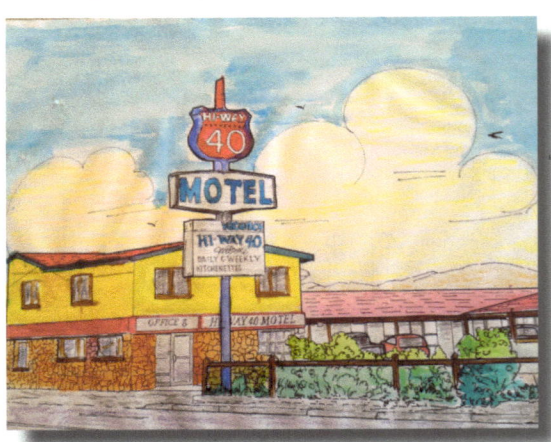

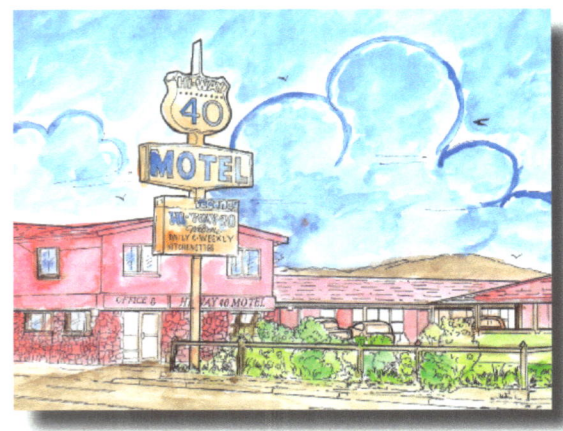

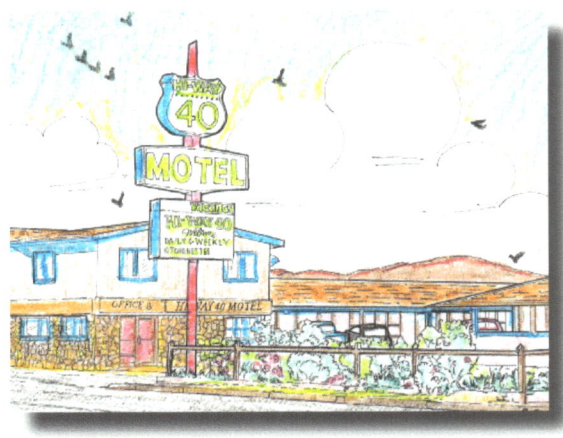

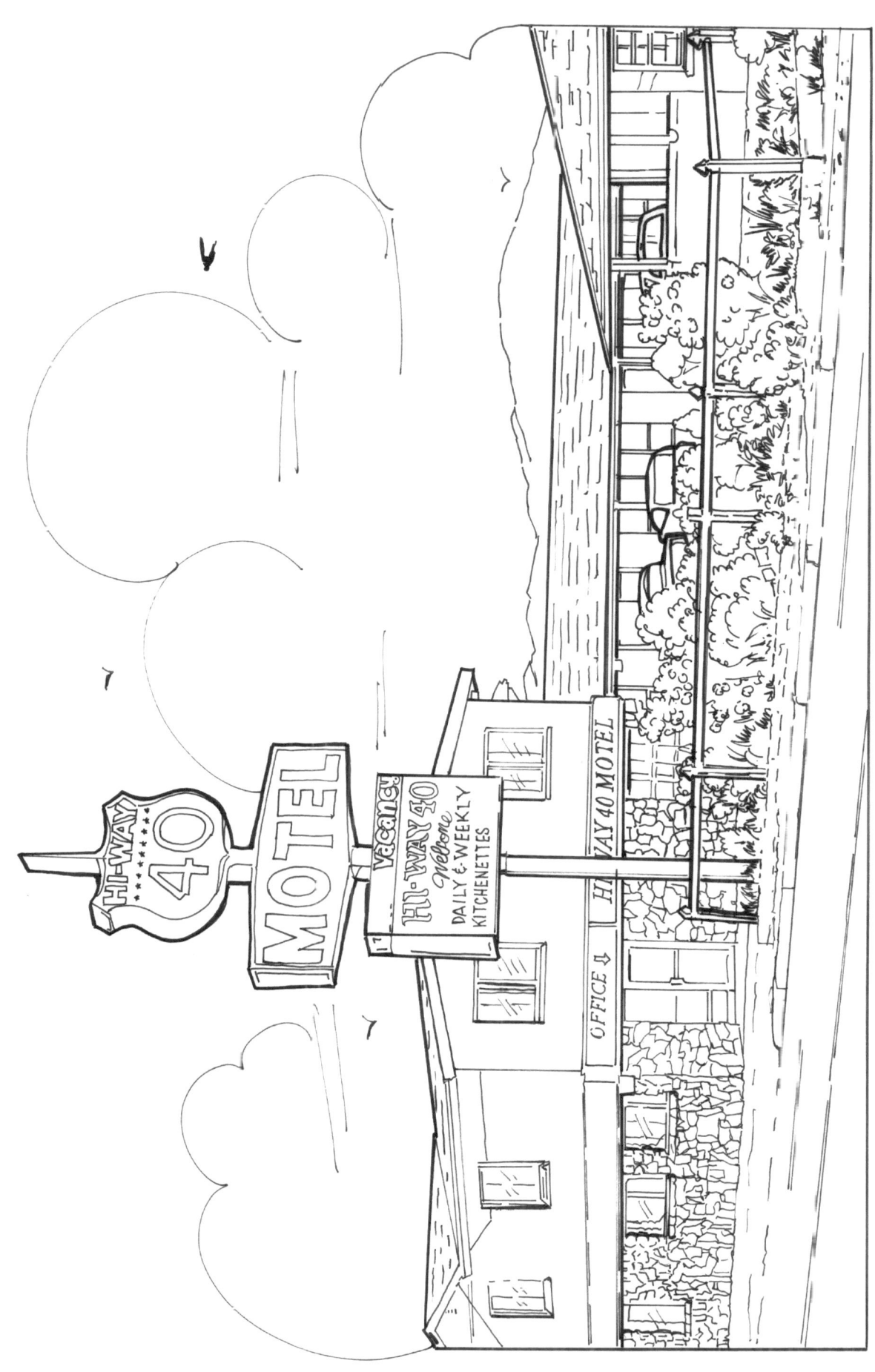

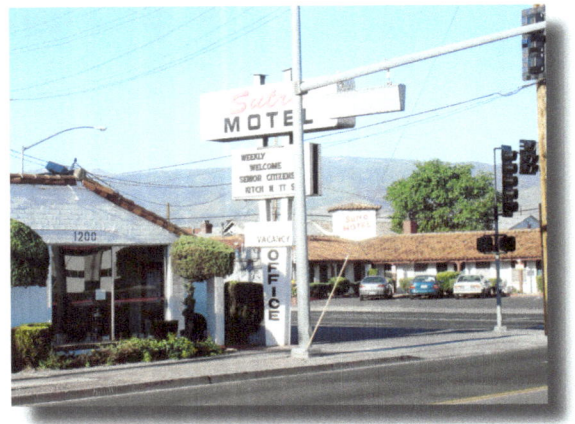

Sutro Motel

Sutro Motel's architectural design is circa 1951.

This property is at
1200 E. Fourth St., Reno

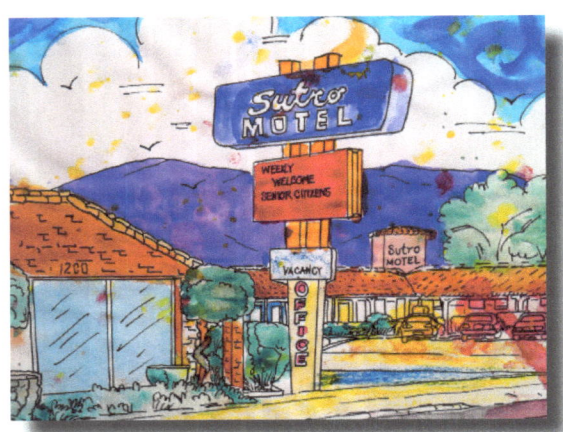

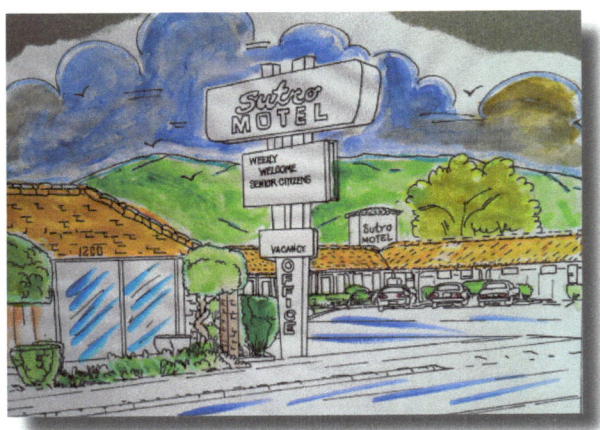

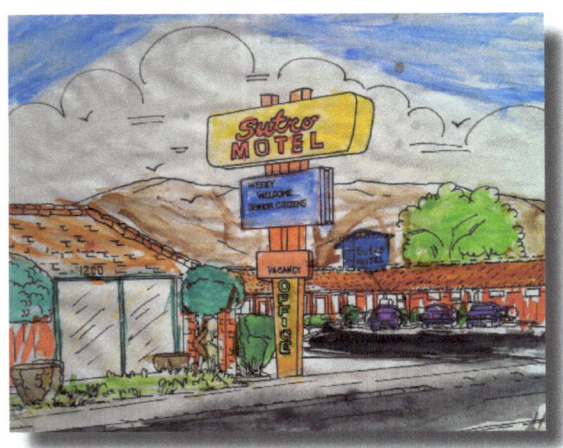

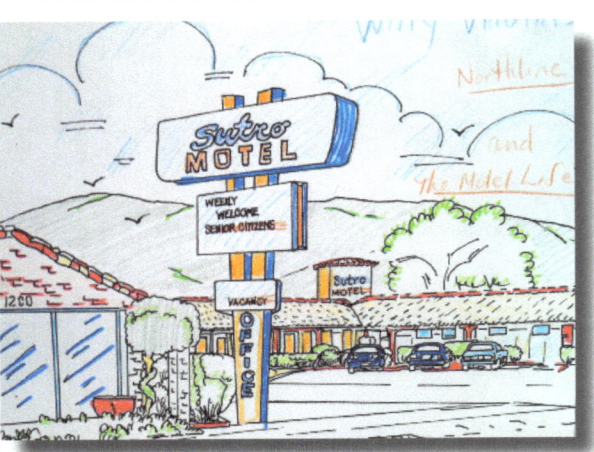

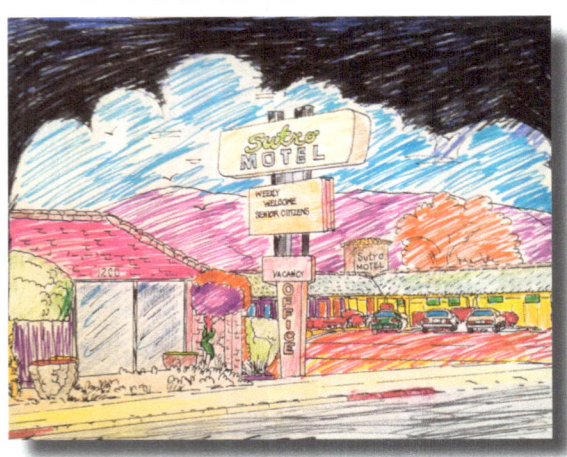

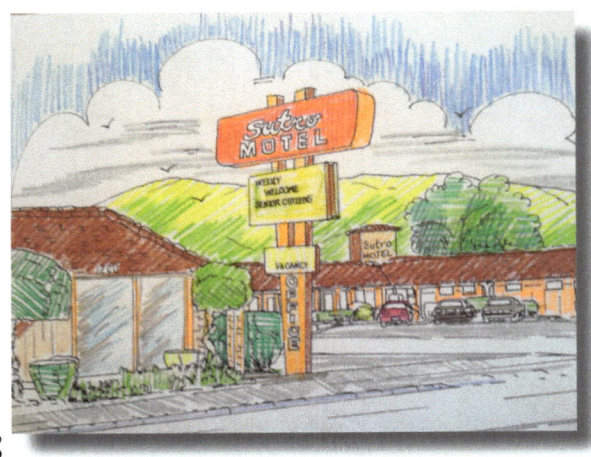

18

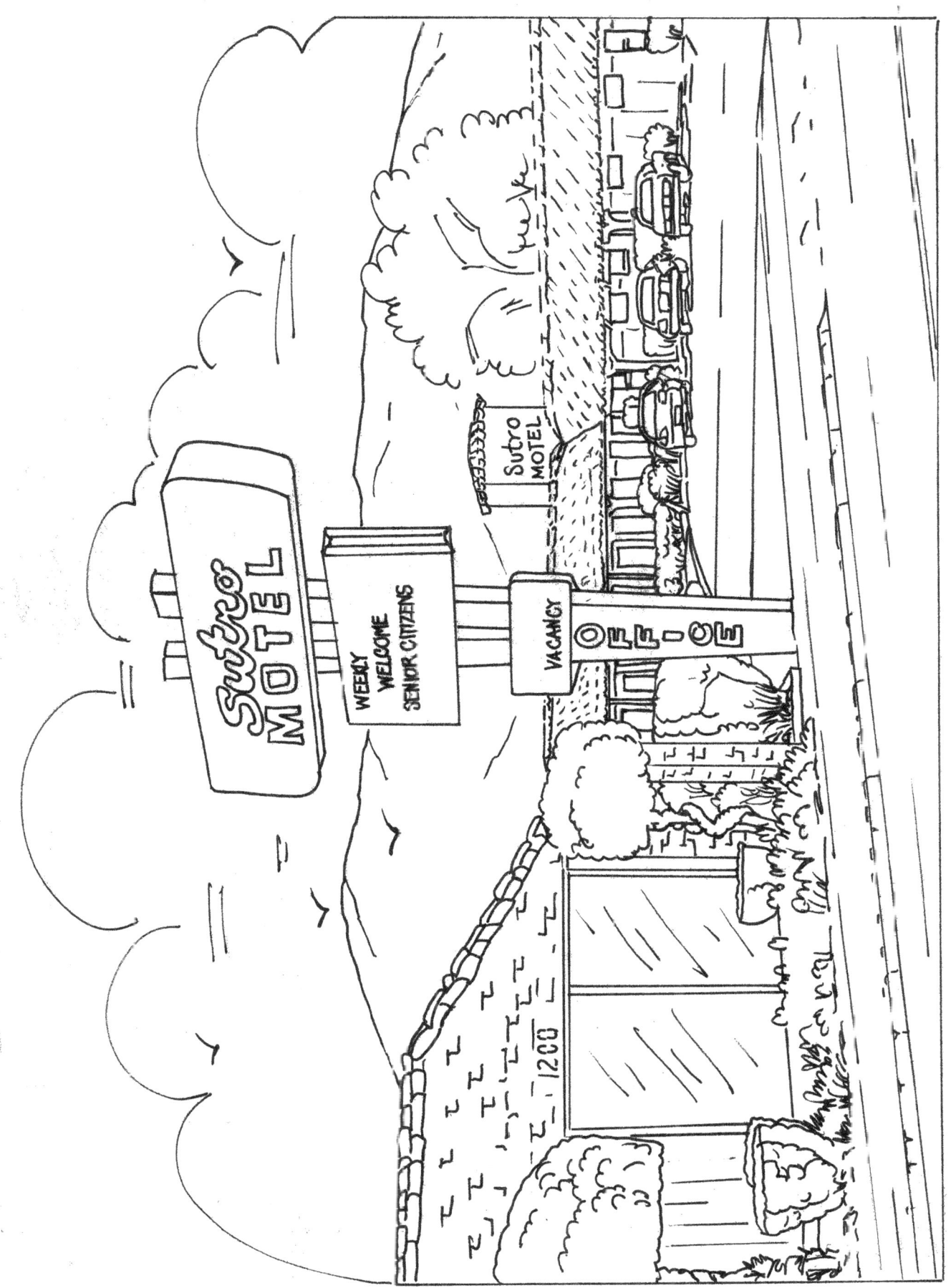

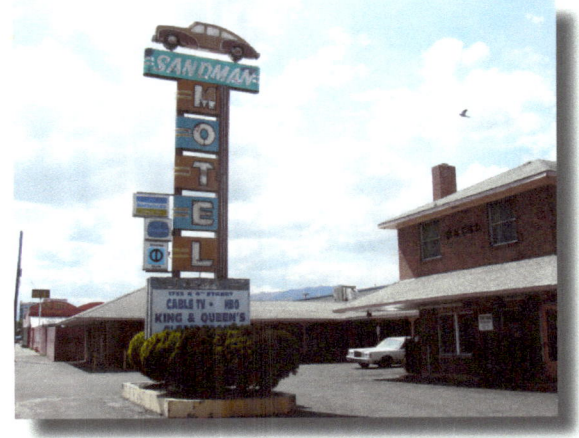

Sandman Motel

Sandman Motel's architectural design is circa 1949.

This property is at
1755 E. Fourth St., Reno

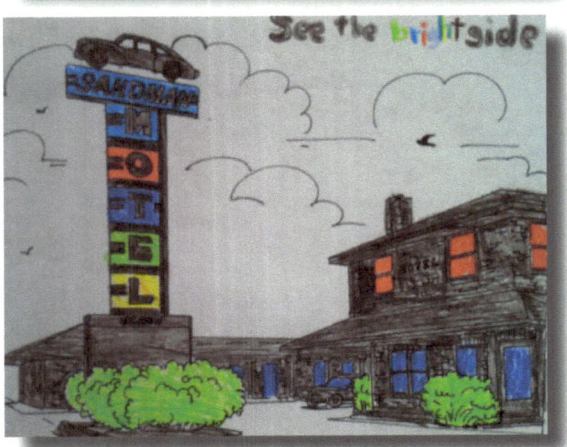

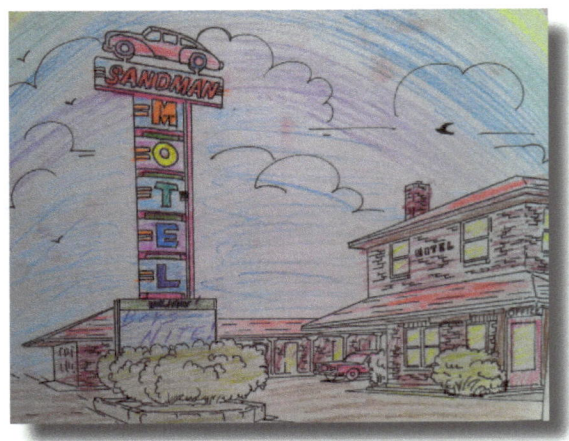

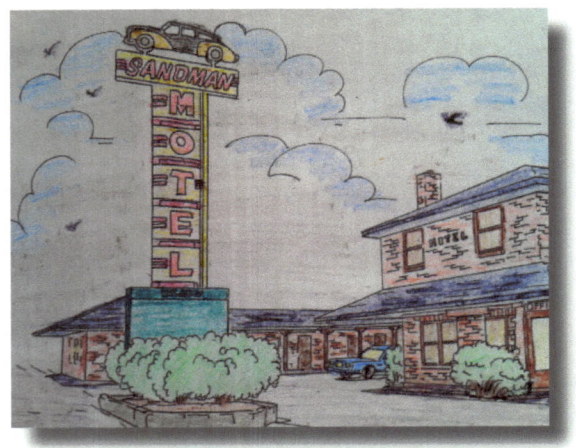

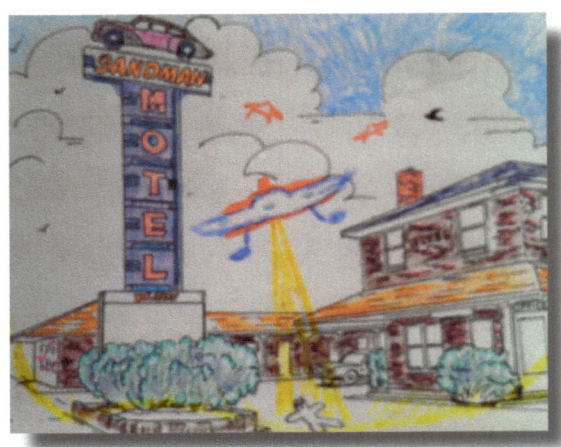

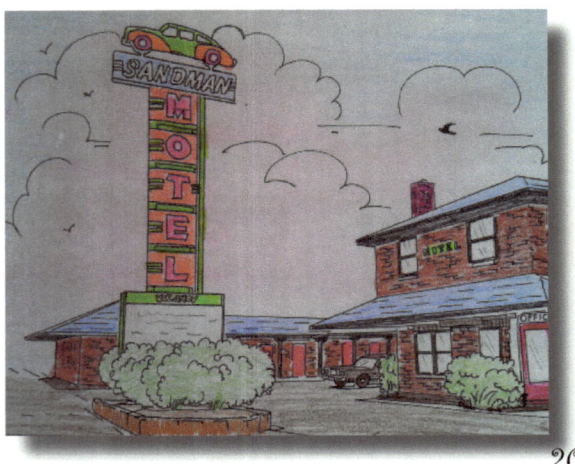

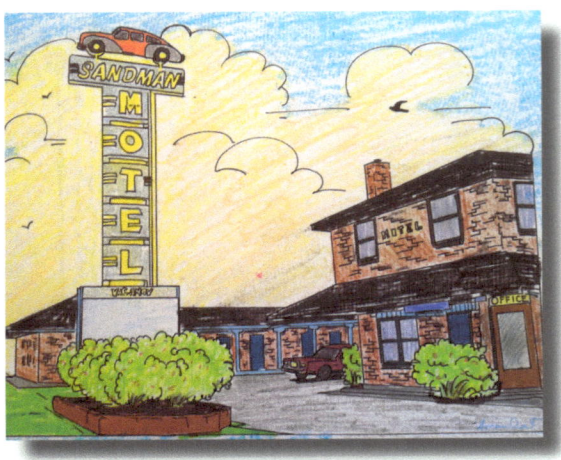

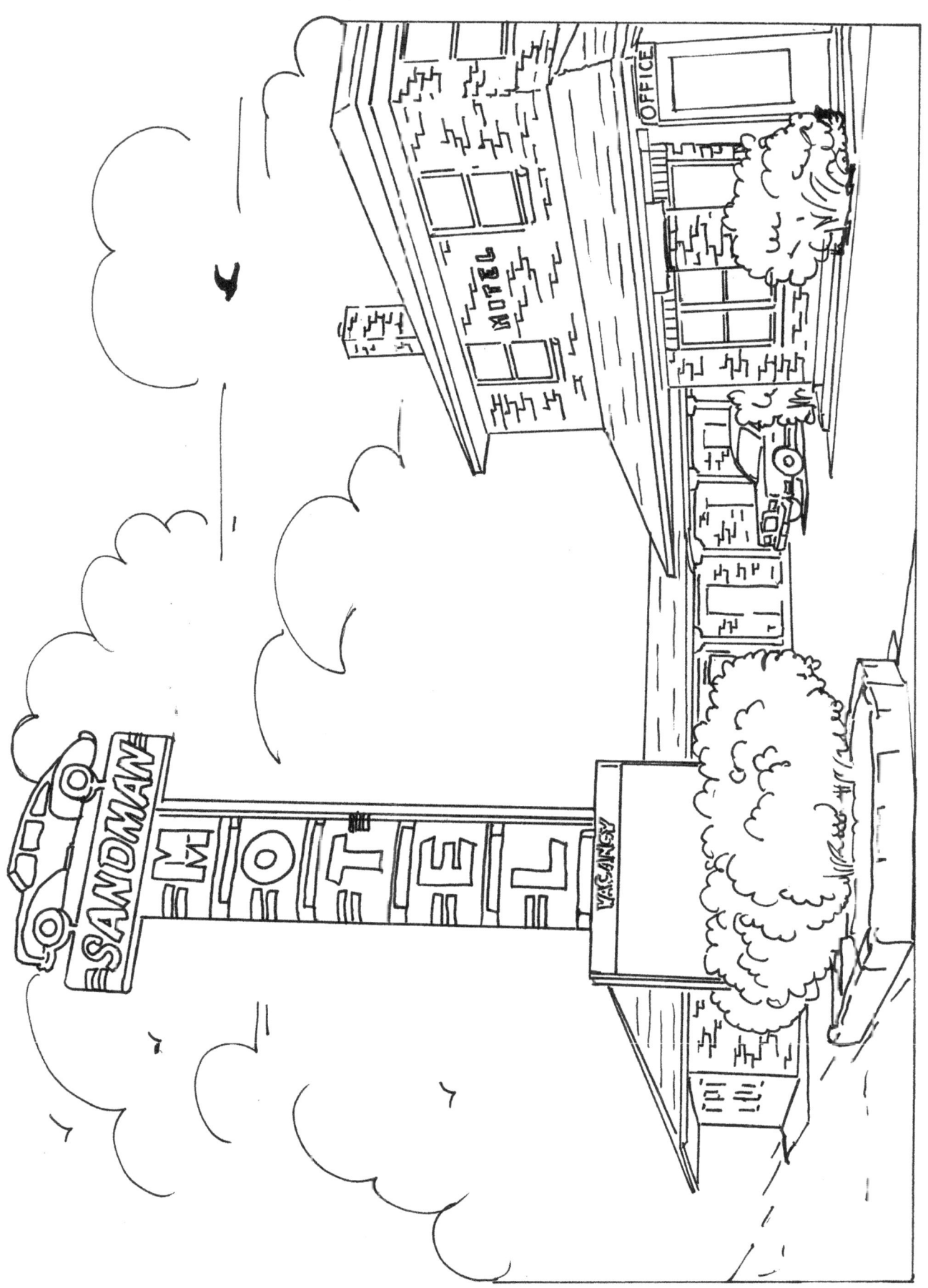

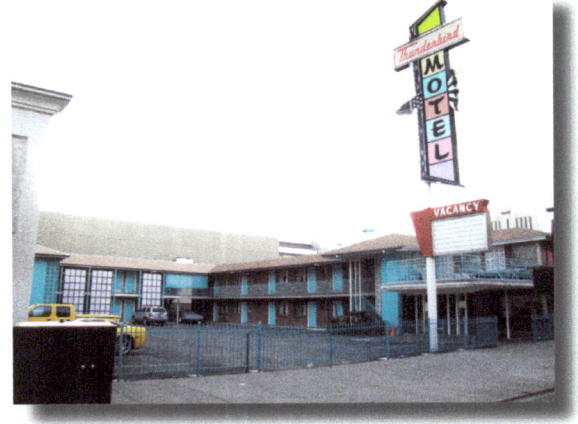

Thunderbird Motel

Thunderbird Motel's architectural design is circa 1958.

This property is at
420 N. Virginia St., Reno

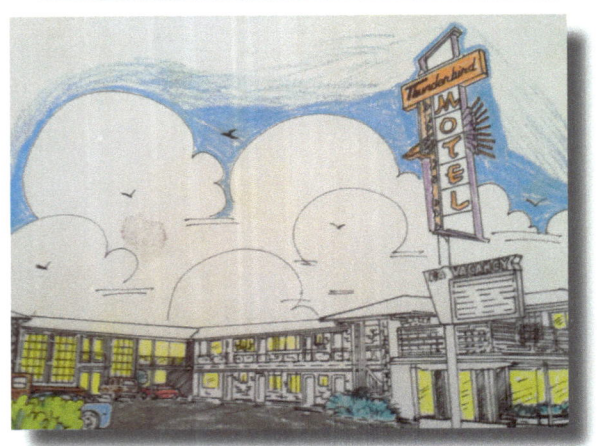

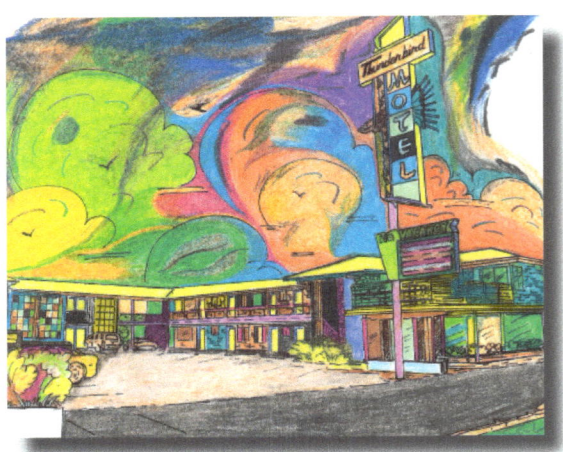

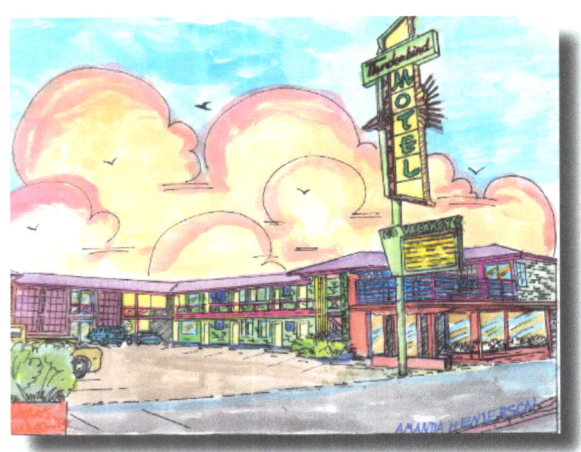

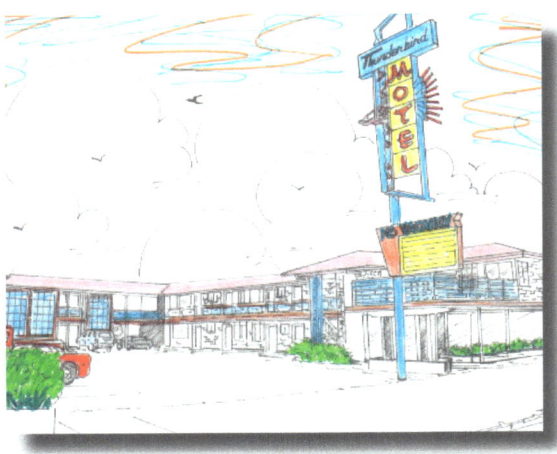

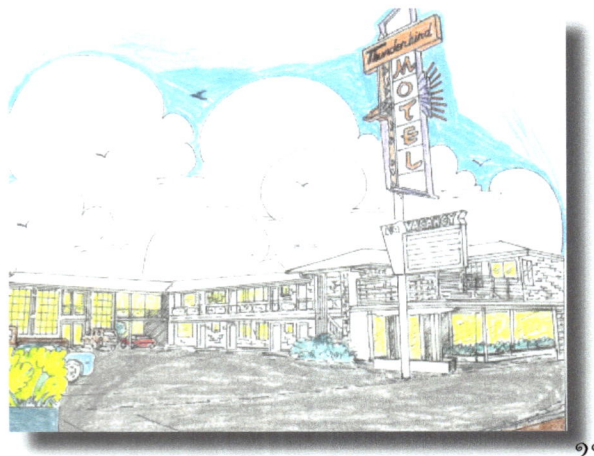

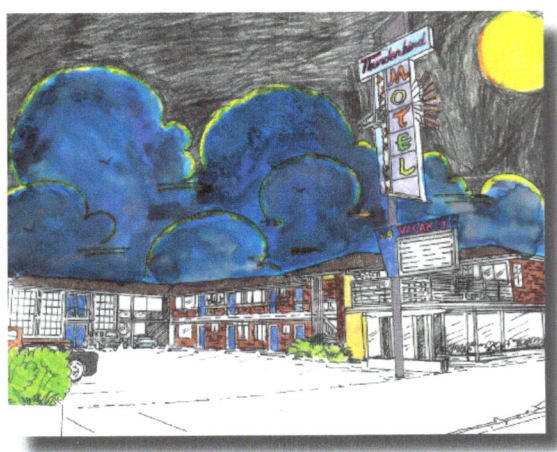

22

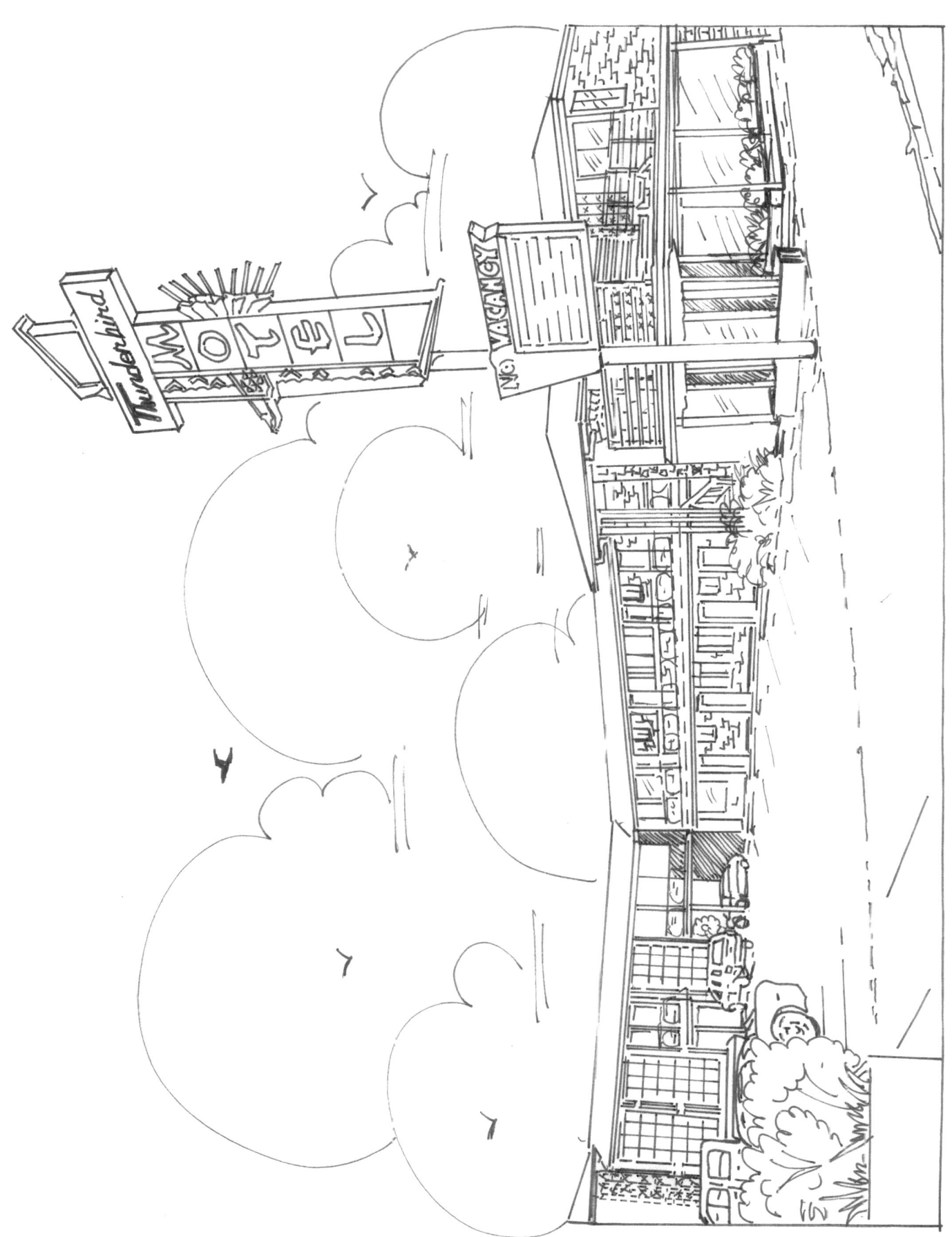

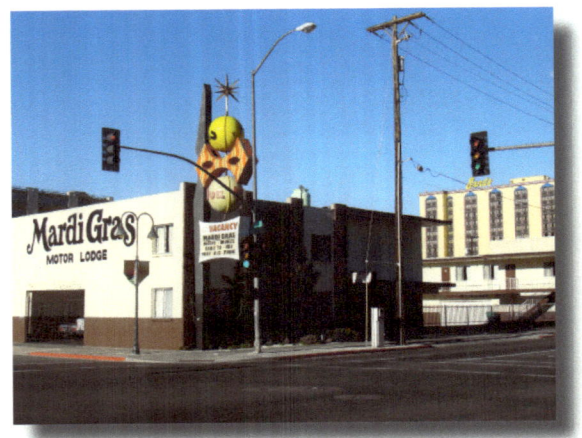

Mardi Gras Motor Lodge

The Mardi Gras Motor Lodge architectural design is circa 1964.

This property is at 200 W. Fourth St., Reno

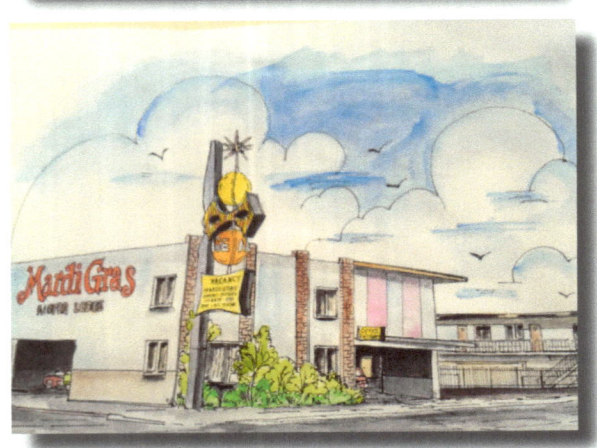

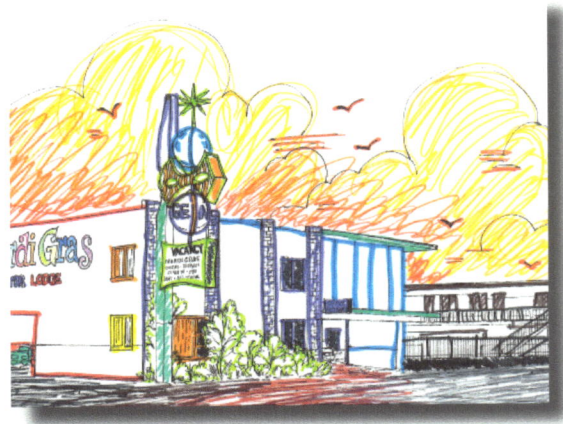

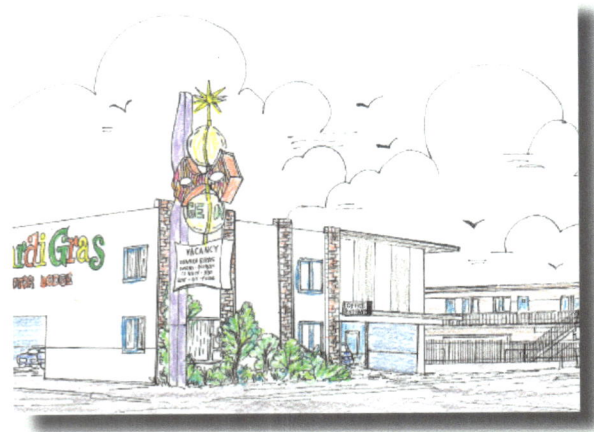

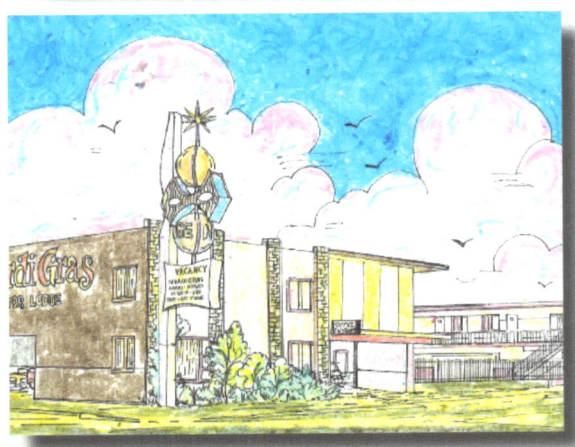

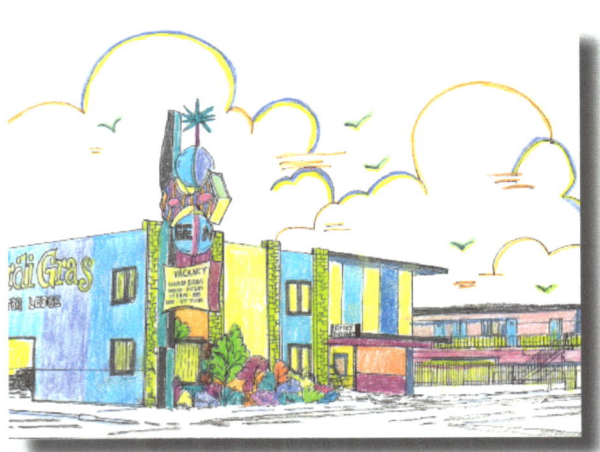

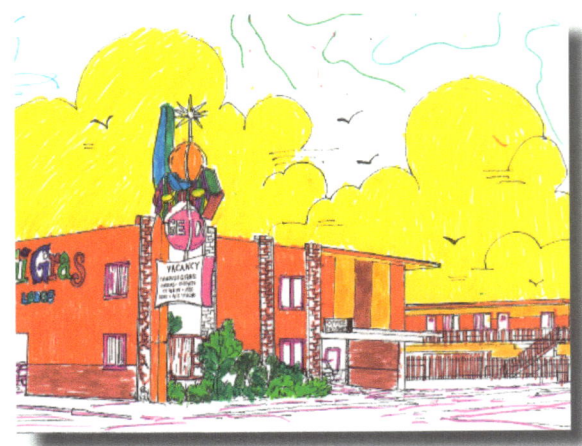

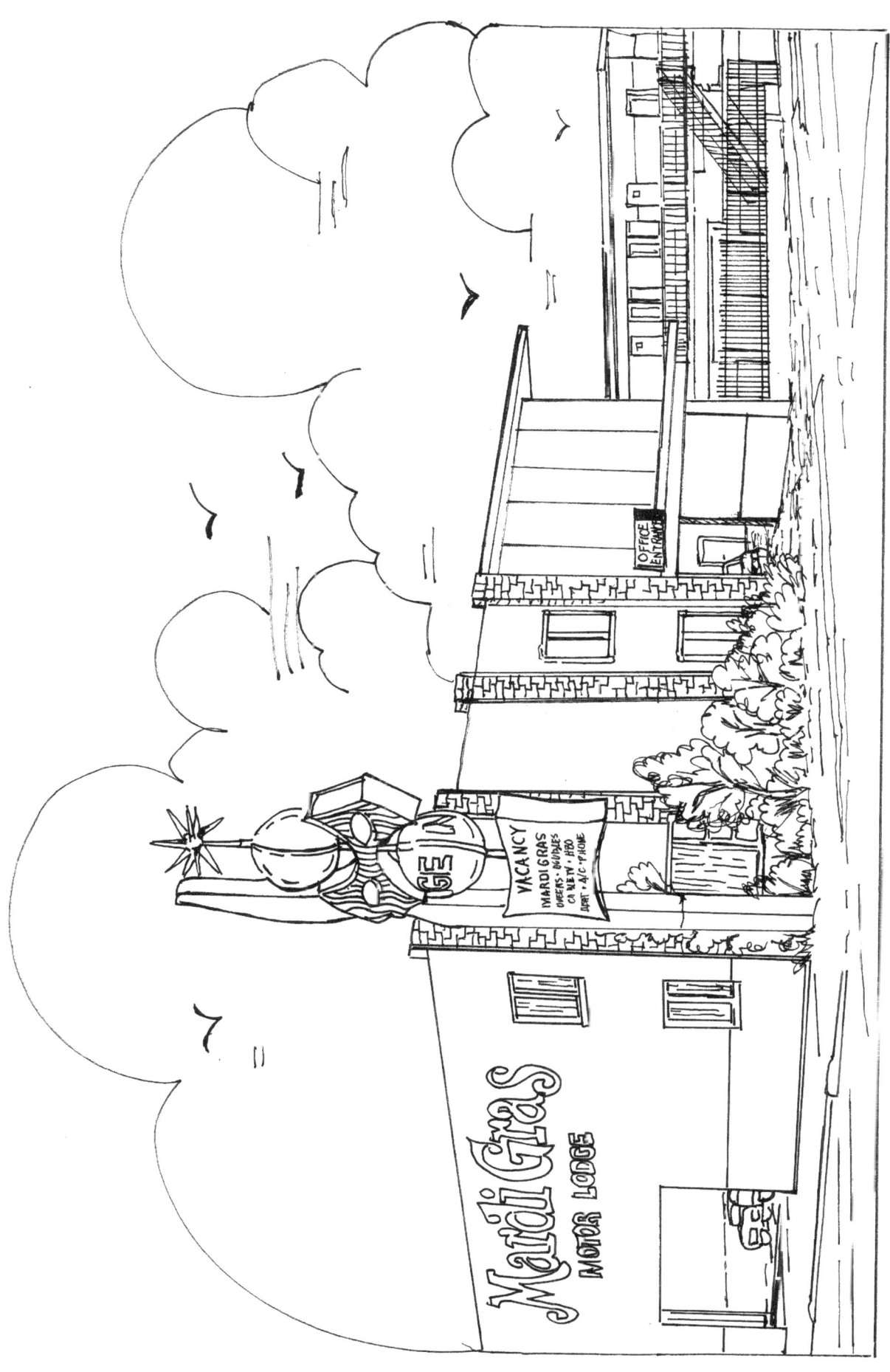

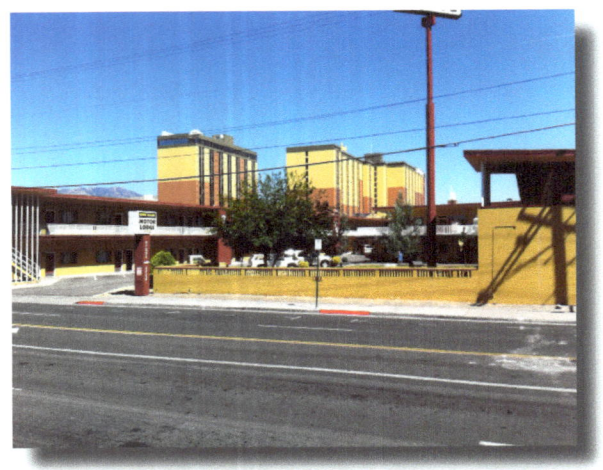

Town House Motor Lodge

The Town House Motor Lodge architectural design is circa 1956.

This property is at
303 W. 2nd St., Reno

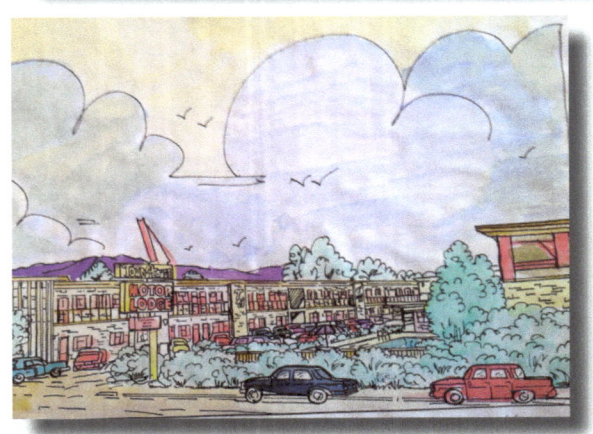

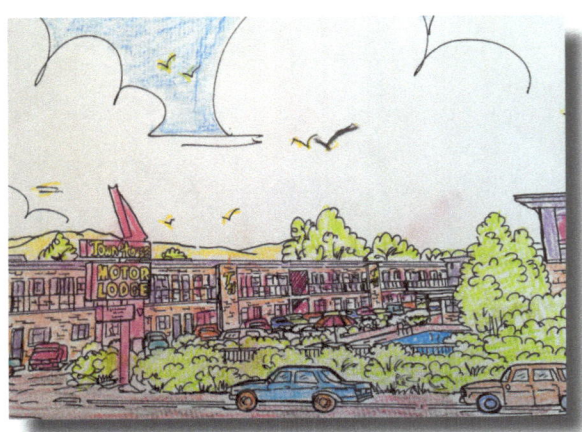

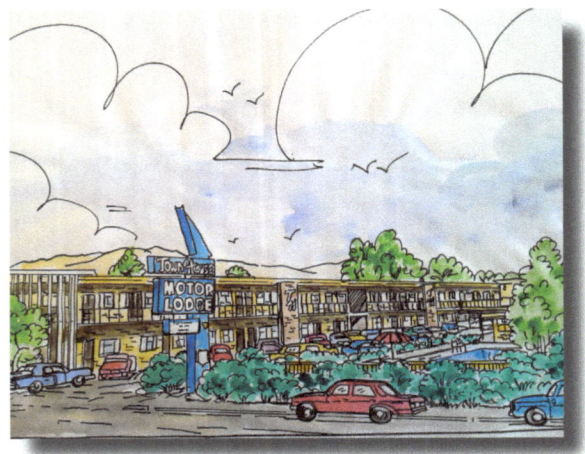

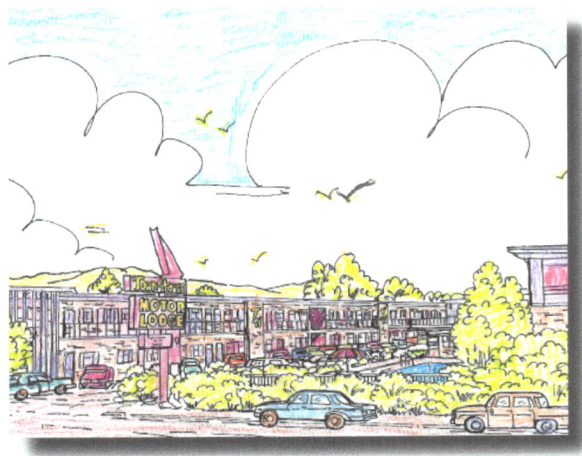

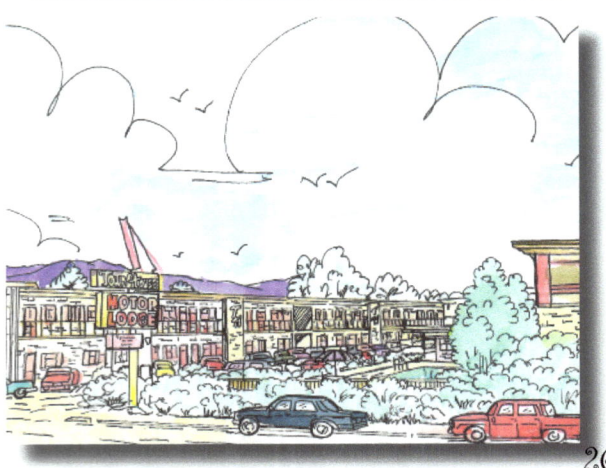

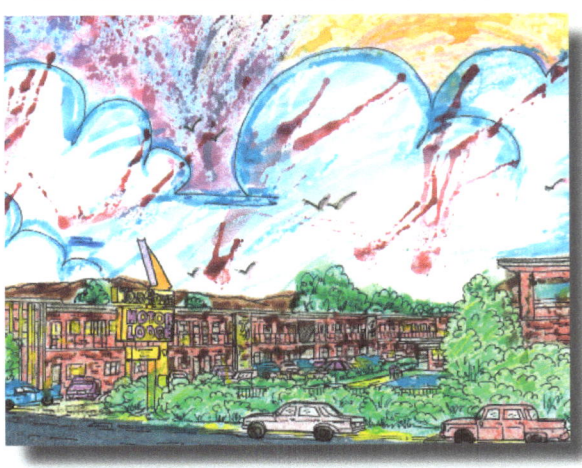

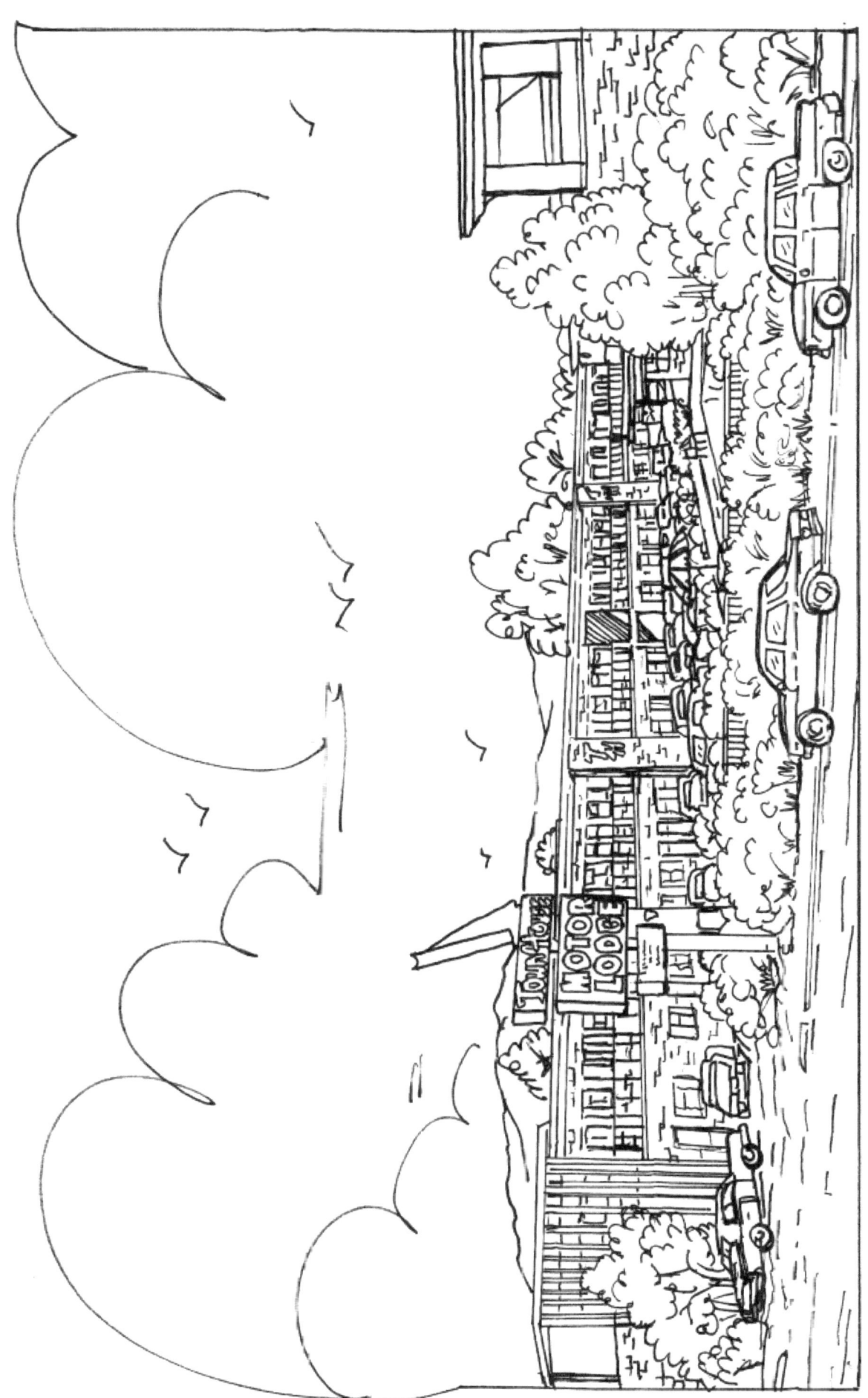

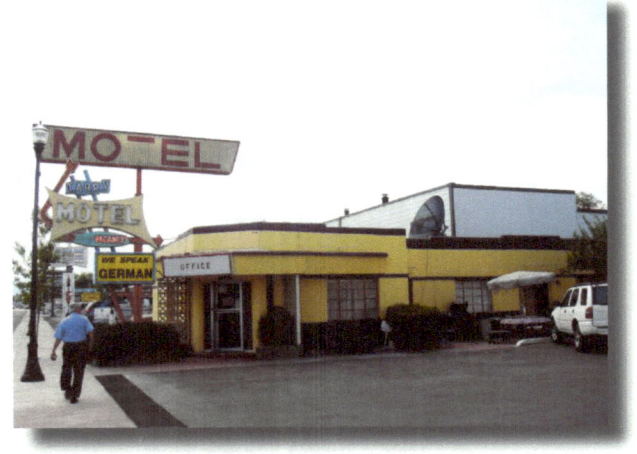

Tarry Motel

The Tarry Motel's
architectural design is circa 1948.

This property is at
1828 Victorian Ave., Sparks

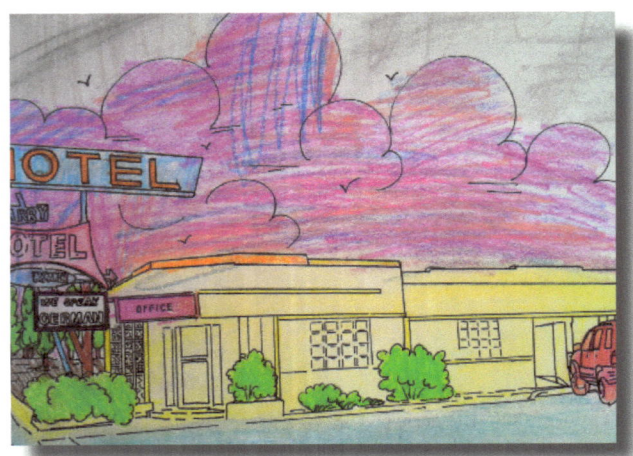

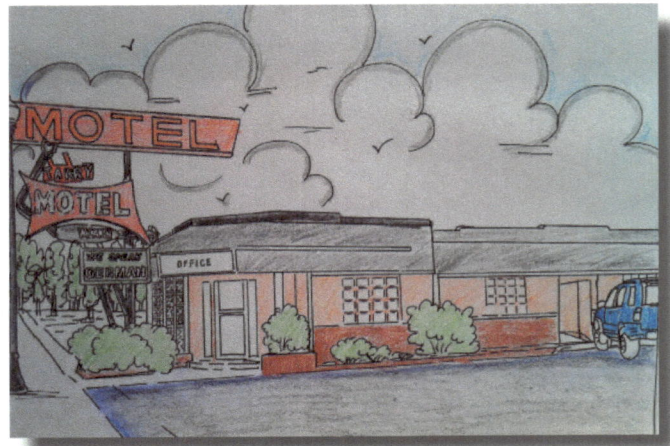

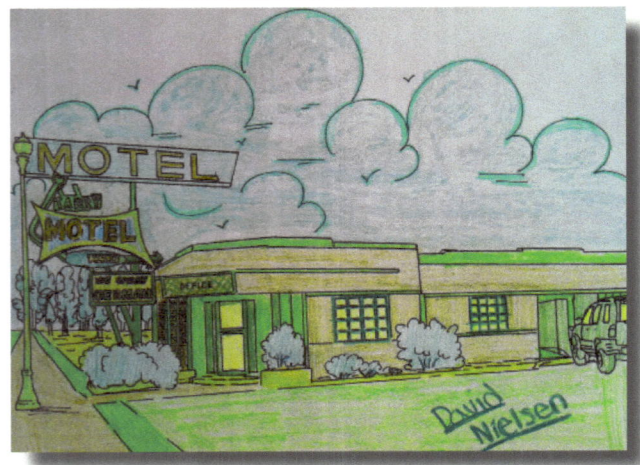

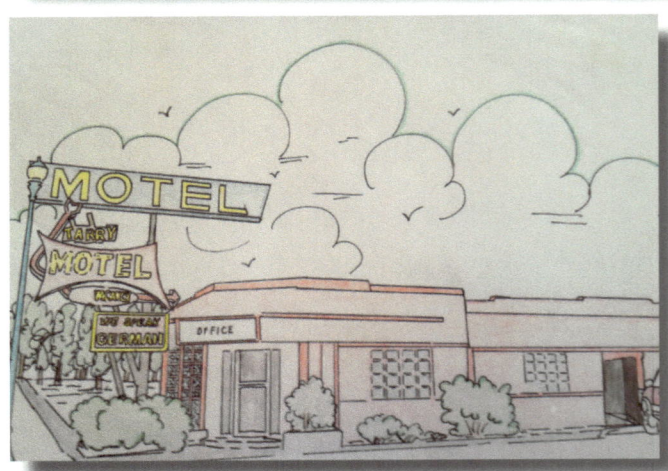

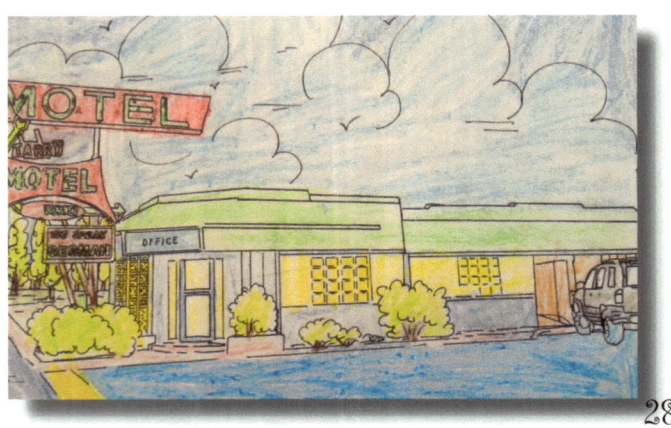

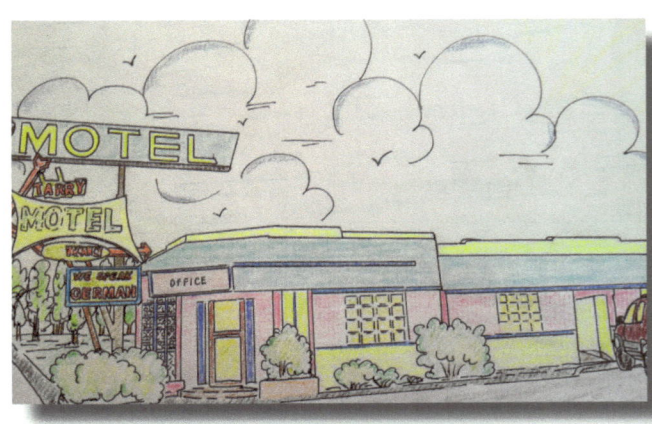

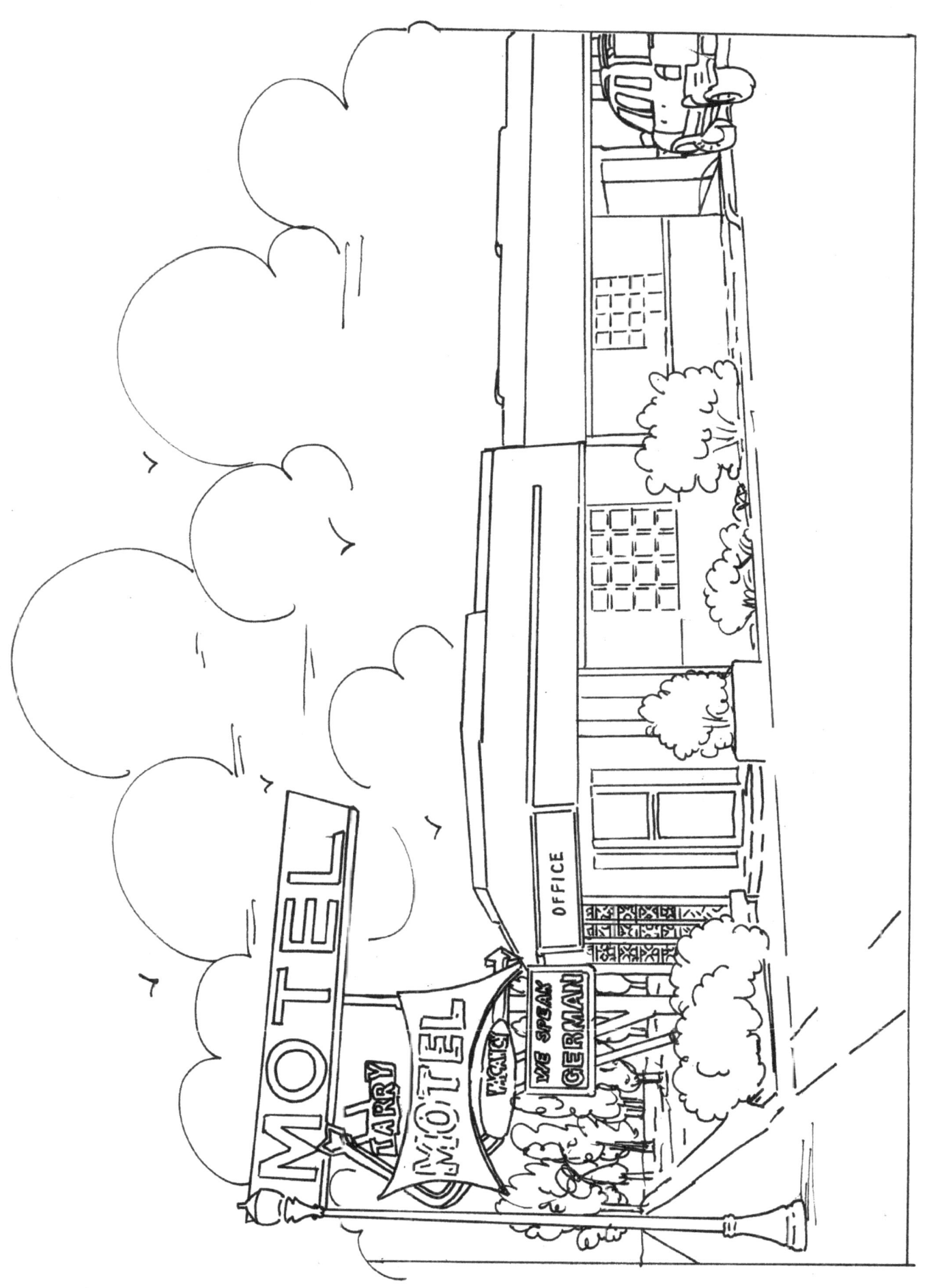

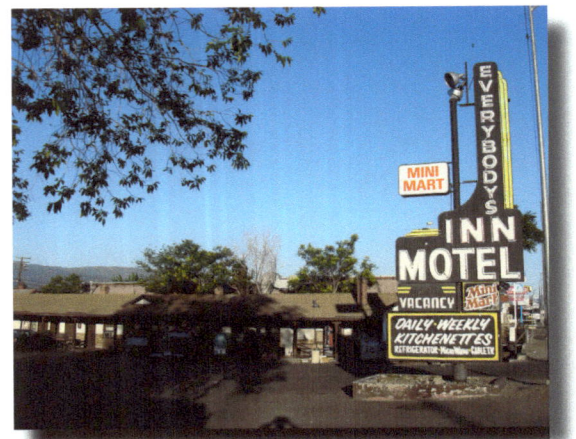

Everybody's Inn

Everybody's Inn's archetectural design is circa 1930.

This property is at
1756 E. Fourth St., Reno

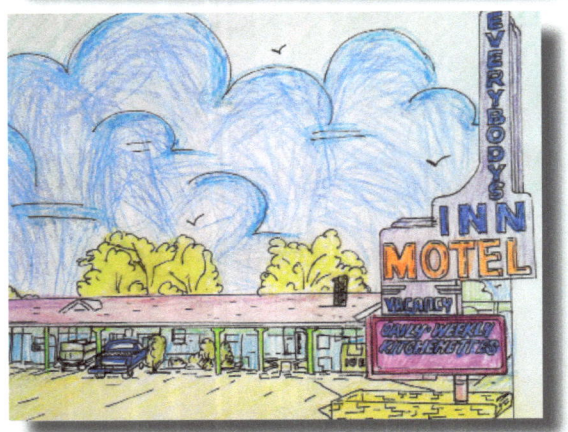
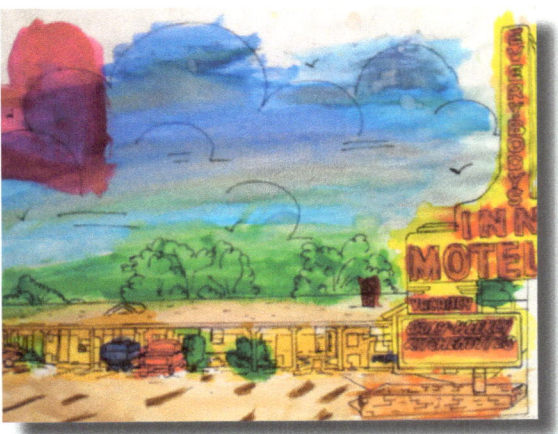

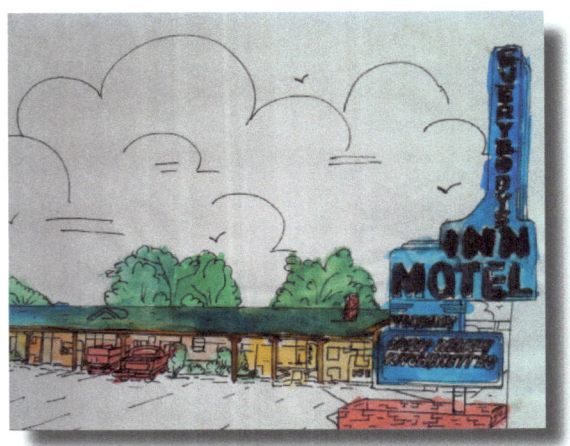
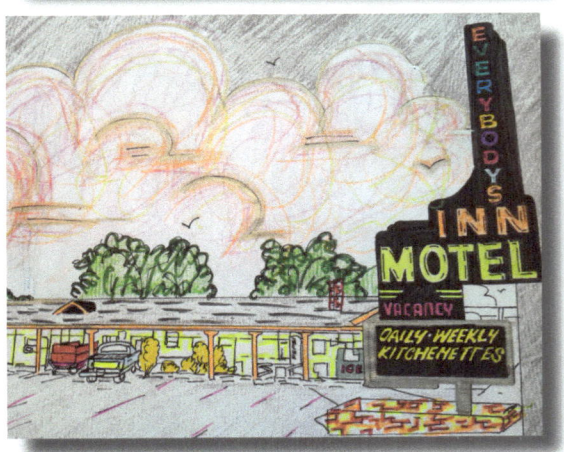

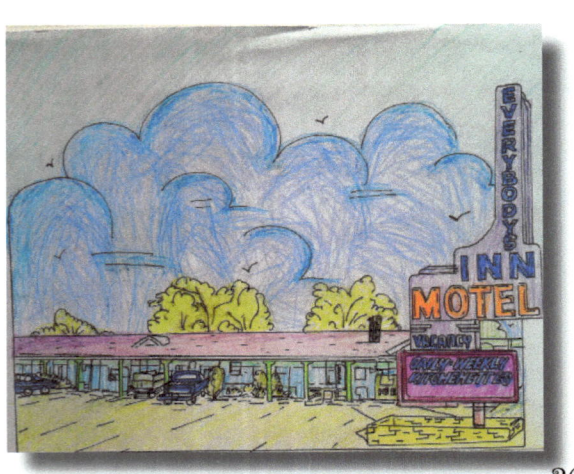
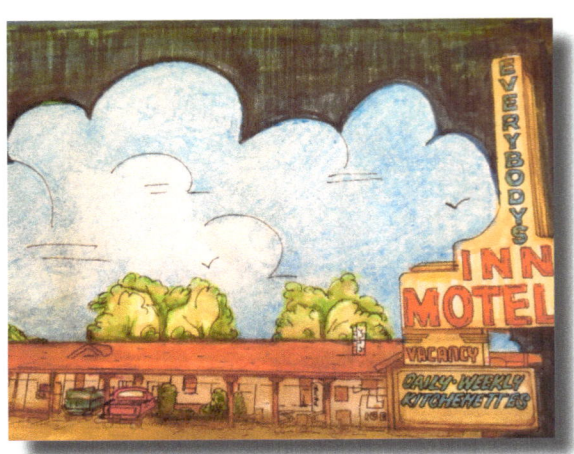

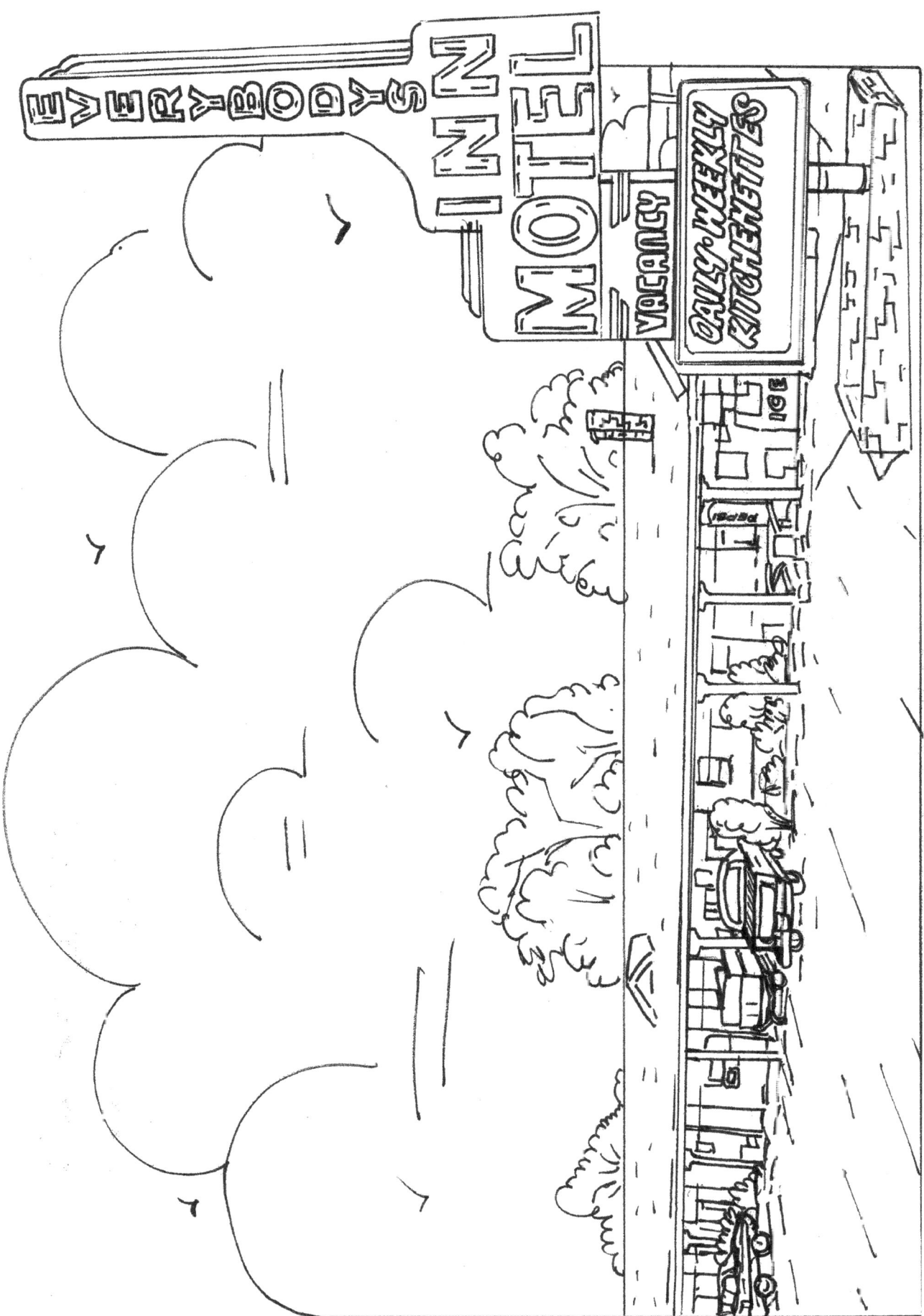

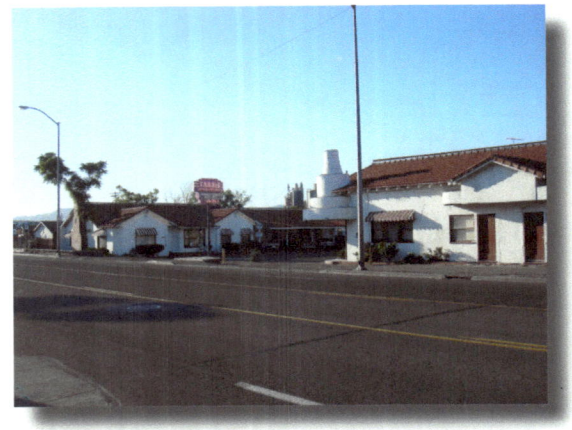

Farris Apartments

The Farris Apartments
archetectural design is circa 1949.

This property is at
1752 E. Fourth St., Reno

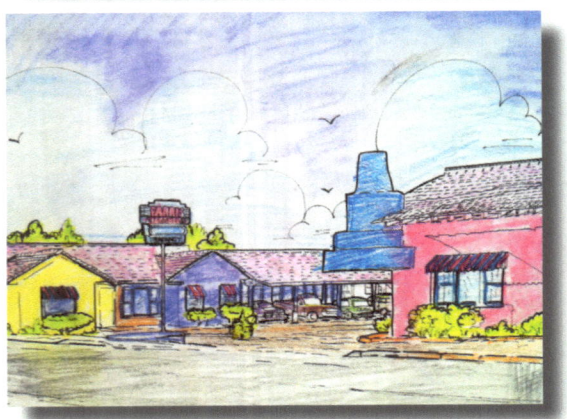

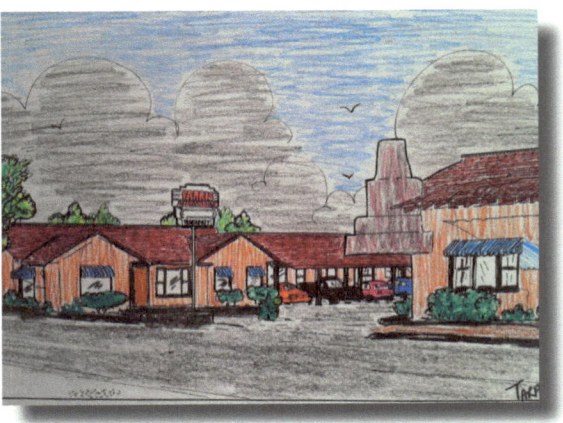

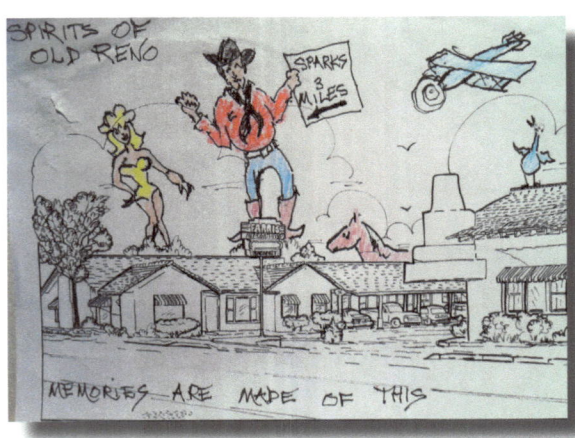

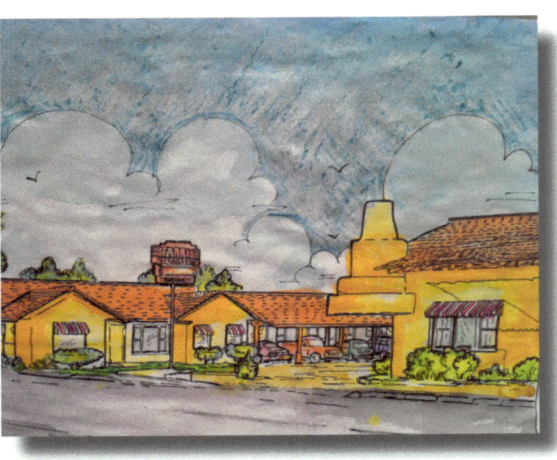

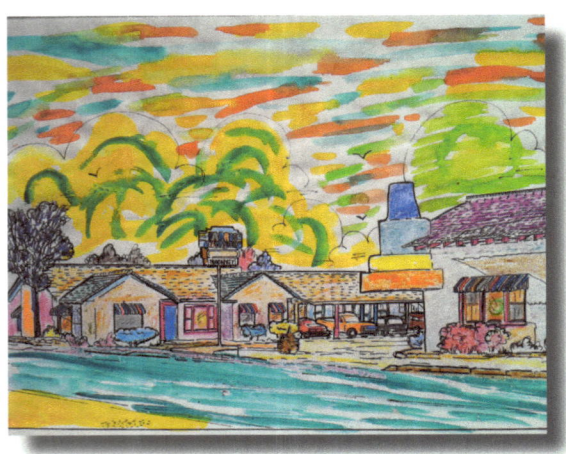

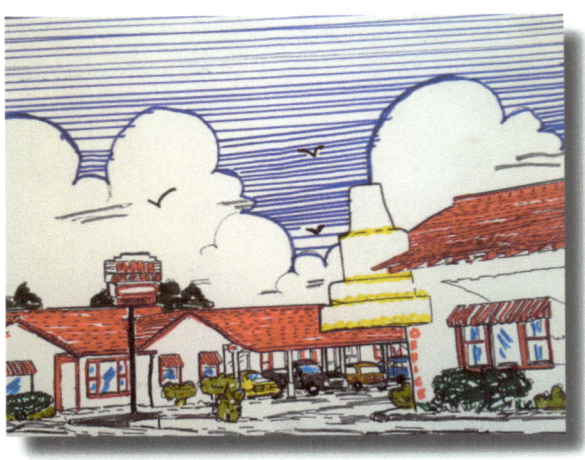

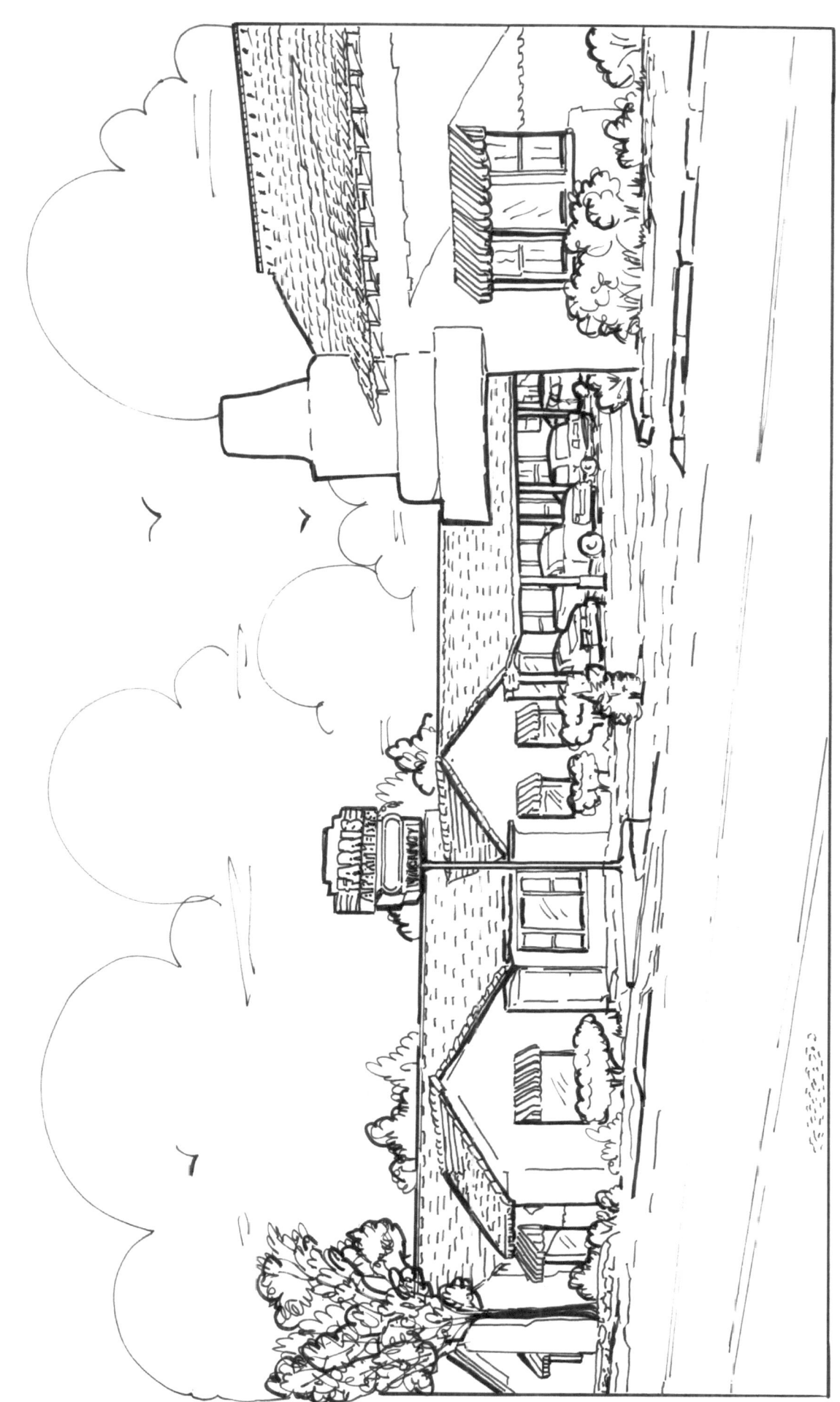

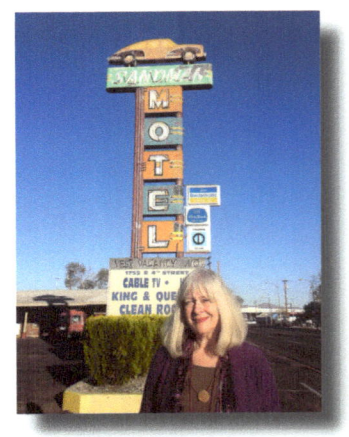

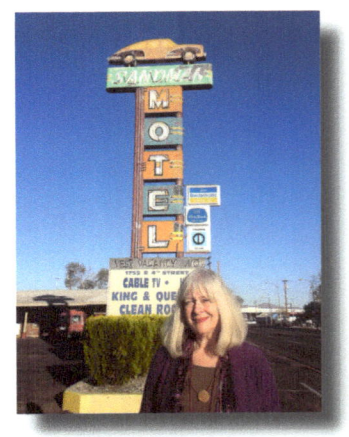

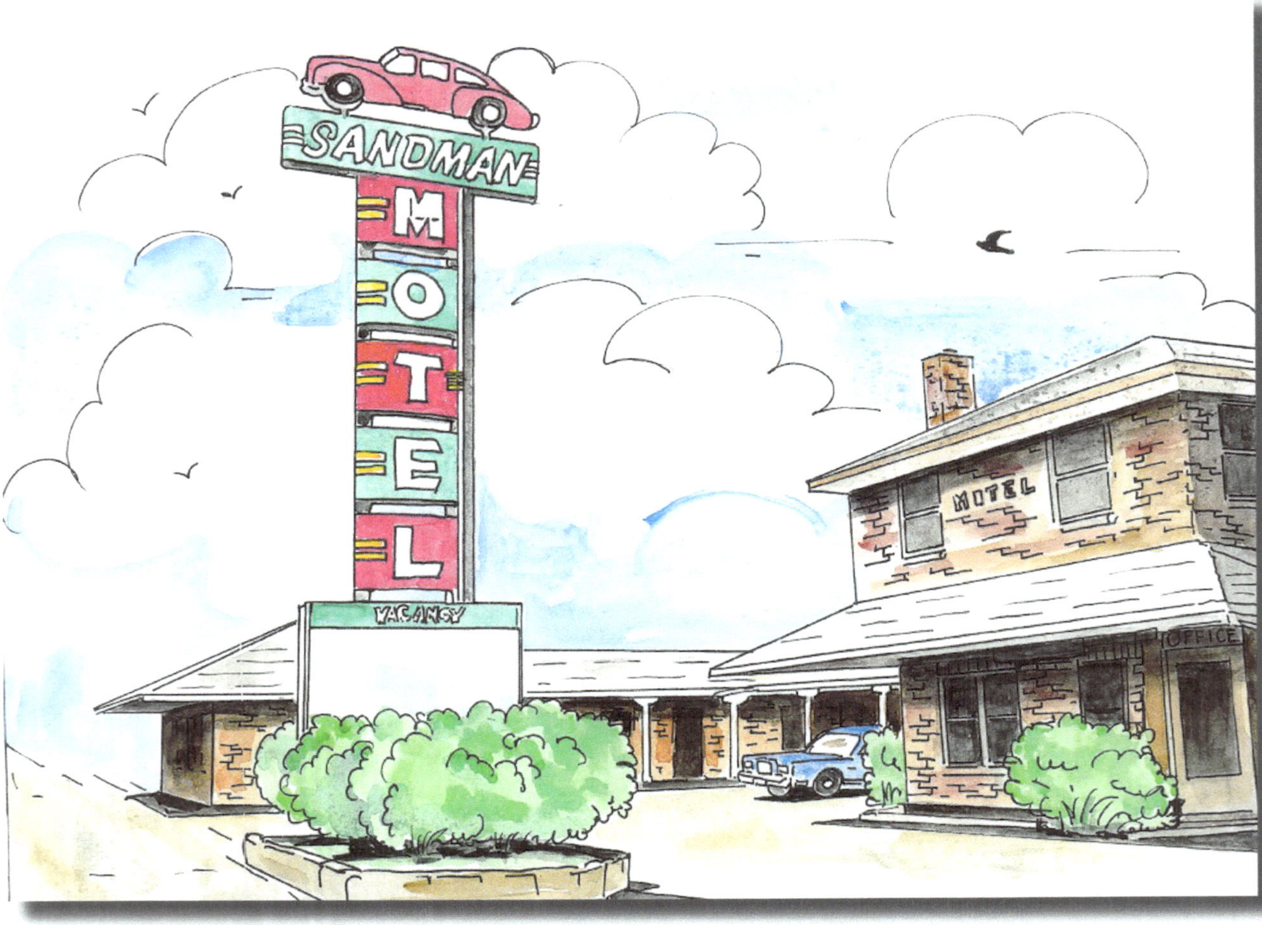

Patty's coloring of the Sandman Motel

NadaDada, Motels and Me
Patty Atcheson Melton

Go ahead!

Get out your color crayons and "have fun" coloring within this publication.

Yes, whether you're still a child, or an adult remaining blessed with the boundless, endlessly creative heart of a youngster, feel free to enjoy generating your own unique masterpiece within these pages. Take delight in coloring these classic motels.

For participants who are adults today, perhaps you remember innocent times from long ago. If you were among the lucky, maybe growing up any time from the 1940s through the 1980s, your teachers or relatives encouraged you to dabble in such art.

Maybe your earliest coloring books featured animals like Bambi or characters such as Hansel and Gretel, Little Red Riding Hood, or any number of additional characters popular among children.

Back then more than a half century ago I lacked any inkling whatsoever deep down in my innocent, boundless heart that someday I would create a coloring book featuring images of the type of unique motels that my family frequently stayed in at the time.

As the person who created and illustrated this coloring book, today I fondly remember enjoying such memorable and heart-warming creative, artistic activities throughout my early childhood. Primarily through the 1950s during my formative years, my late mother, Angel's Camp, California, native Audrey Chisholm Edwards encouraged me to draw and to fill coloring books.

Throughout much of that period we intermittently lived in countless motels throughout much of the western United States. My late father, J Lawrence "Lucky Larry" Edwards, a native of Filer, Idaho, worked as a body-and-fender man, driving his wife and two small children from town to town so that he could continually land work repairing cars.

Where Are All The
MAGPIES

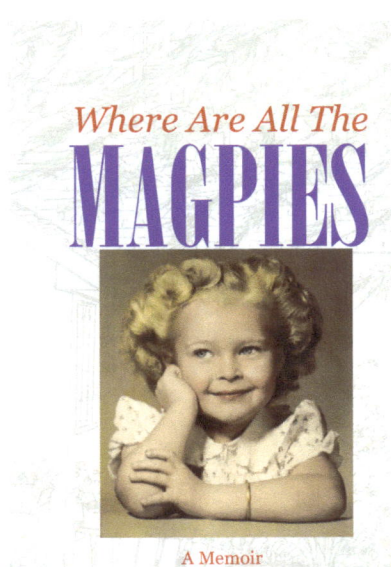

A Memoir
Patty Atcheson Melton

Until around my 10th birthday we stayed in so many motels that today, all these many years later, I fail to remember them all. Even so, I managed to chronicle lots of these tales in my 2012 memoir, "Where Are All The Magpies," which you can find at Reno's Sundance Books and Music and on Amazon.com.

My husband Wayne Rollan Melton exaggerates a bit when he occasionally tells people that "my wife essentially grew up in the front seat of a pickup truck."

Yet in a sense such observations are somewhat close to the proverbial bull's eye. Back then, the chain motels that most of us are familiar with today did not exist—the likes of Holiday Inn, Motel 6, La Quinta and so many others.

Unlike today, the vast majority of motels from the late 1940s until the late 1950s were independently owned rather than part of national or international corporate chains. Most motels then featured unique designs, ranging from buildings that looked like hats or shoes to facilities embossed with themes such as Western cowboy styles, Native American or European.

Of course, I had little inkling back then that the era would eventually become perceived much later during the 21st century as "those innocent times of long ago." Indeed, back then people staying at most motels in the mid-twenteith century often got to know each other through relaxed, informal and friendly chit-chat. That's a sharp contrast to today as just about everyone feels a burning need to approach strangers with great suspicion or most preferably to avoid them.

Back then I never saw a motel check-in counter surrounded by security gates or bars. Round-the-clock video surveillance and automatic alarms at the time were a figment of the imagination.

A happy-go-lucky, rambunctious child with boundless enthusiasm, I continually drew or used color crayons while sitting inside the pickup truck with my family amid these lengthy, seemingly endless excursions. Each motel we visited had its own unique design, theme and atmosphere—every one of these first-time excursions unlike other motels we had previously visited.

Anyone under age 40 today might have a difficult time envisioning this. Yet it's true. You see, prior to the late 1950s and early 1960s, the USA lacked the gargantuan interstate highway system that people today take for granted. Prior to this development instituted by President Dwight David Eisenhower's administration, the vast majority of U.S. highways were mere two-lane roads—one lane in each direction.

Although continually enrolled in new schools as we moved at a relentless pace, coloring books and artwork remained among the few constant, reliable and fairly predictable activities in my young life.

My heart and soul also got a sense of fulfillment, filling my coloring books and sketch pads while on motel room floors, atop the beds in such facilities or on any available countertop.

In the process I developed unique skills that enabled me as an adult to become a graphic designer and a skilled commission-based portrait artist.

My early experiences living intermittently in motels remained an integral part of my soul when becoming art director for the California Chamber of Commerce during my early 20s in the 1970s, then based in Sacramento.

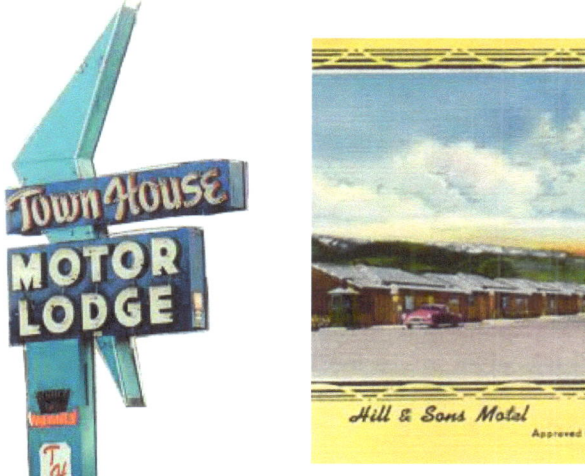 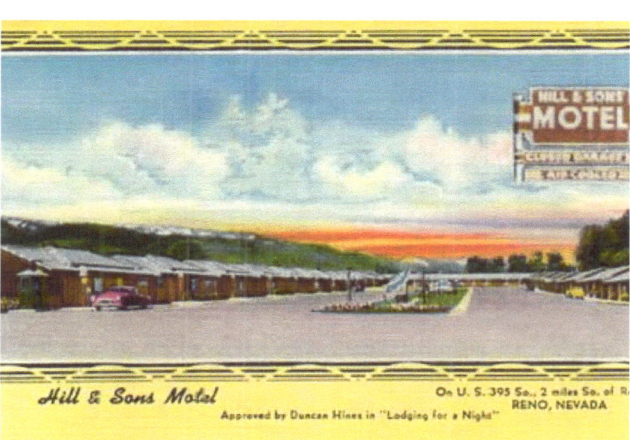

Hill & Sons Motel
On U.S. 395 So., 2 miles So. of R.
RENO, NEVADA
Approved by Duncan Hines in "Lodging for a Night"

Only a handful of my many friends at the time realized my unique history, including the fact that my grandparents, Geneva and Oscar Hedman, had managed two iconic motels in Reno, Nevada, in the 1950s and 1960s. The former Hill and Sons Motel now gone, the site of the Peppermill Resort Spa Casino, and the Town House Motor Lodge, which still remains in operation today, were among the West's most widely acclaimed facilities of their kind at the time.

One of my most cherished memories remains swimming at about age 13 in around 1960 with then-U.S. Senator Lyndon Baines Johnson of Texas in the Town House pool as he campaigned for the vice presidency, running mate of the successful presidential candidate Senator John Fitzgerald Kennedy of Massachusetts.

Just seven years later in 1967 while a 20-year-old newly married mother of a newborn, I landed my first professional artist job working as a fashion illustrator at the former Gray Reid's department store in Reno. Blessed with boundless energy and increasingly eager for continued success, soon afterward in the late 1960s I then landed a highly coveted job as the first female artist in the formerly all-male graphics department at the Tyson Curtis Wilson Advertising Agency in Reno.

As previously stated, upon honing my professional skills for several years, in the early 1970s I became the first female art director for the California Chamber of Commerce in Sacramento, where I had moved with my

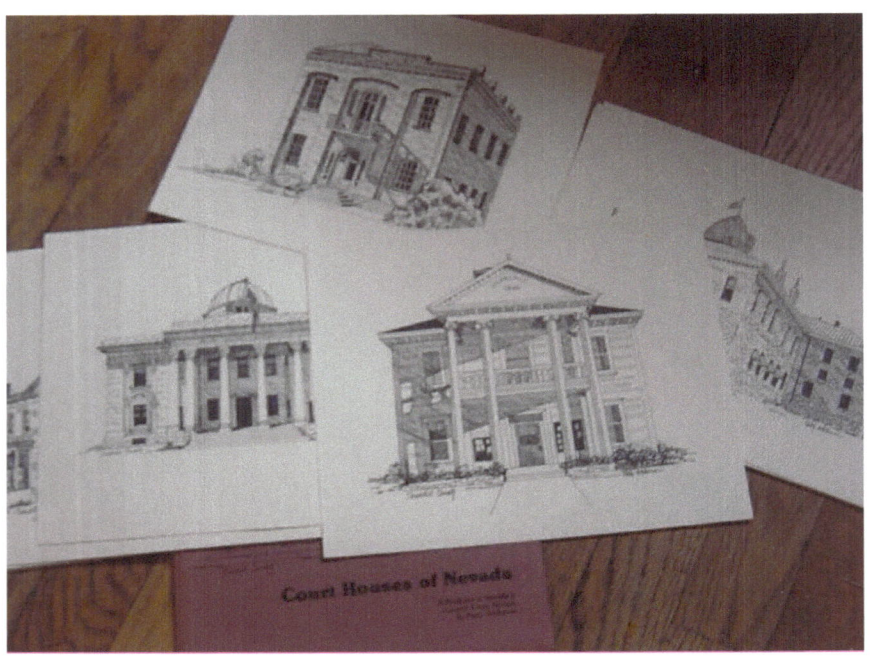

My pen and ink drawings for a limited edition of 200 portfolios of the seventeen county court houses of the State of Nevada was part of the inspiration to produce the motel pen and ink drawings.

then-husband Fred Hill Atcheson so that he could attend McGeorge School of Law in the Golden State's capital city.

Little did I know at the time, of course, that all of my various personal artistic and professional experiences would eventually culminate in this coloring book. Along the way, my many other professional experiences included: art director for the Nevada Department of Tourism and Economic Development in Carson City; a faculty member at the University of Nevada, Reno, specializing in illustration and graphic design in producing numerous magazines, brochures and advertisements.

Encouraged by friends and associates, I created a popular 200 limited-edition portfolio of pen-and-ink illustrations of each of Nevada's 17 individual county courthouses. During the 1980s I became the first graphic designer in Nevada to use computers in creating award-winning designs and illustrations for a steadily growing number of clients.

As the sole owner of a highly successful graphic design business with clients in Reno and Las Vegas, I commuted weekly via jet between these cities during the late 1980s into the mid-1990s.

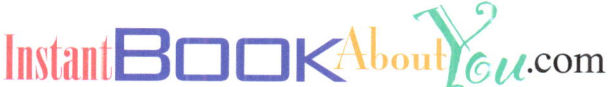

Following my 1996 marriage to Wayne, a journalist, entrepreneur and book ghostwriter, my life took a new course in the 21st century when we launched a book publishing company designed to serve clients worldwide.

All these many blessings blossomed further in around 2005 when my good friend Pat Campbell offered me space for an art studio at her widely acclaimed Wildflower Village facility on West Fourth Street in Reno—comprised of five formerly seedy but now spruced-up old former motels. I still maintain this studio thanks to Pat.

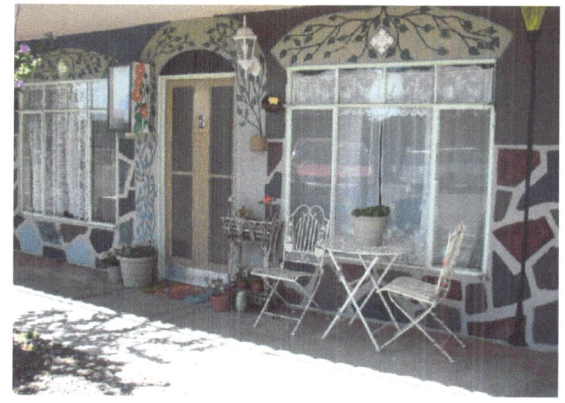
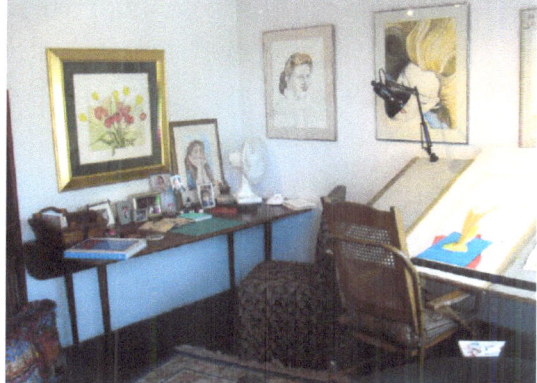

My studo at Wildflwoer Village.

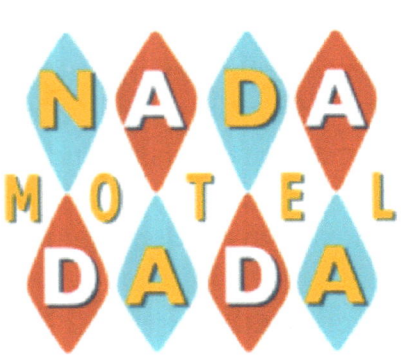 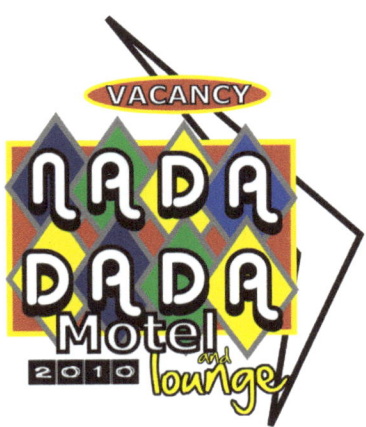

In another stroke of luck near and dear to my heart, in late 2006 six Northwest Nevada artists banded together to create a unique, eclectic art movement called "NadaDada Motel," which soon earned national and international acclaim.

These distinctive and diverse visual artists adopted the "Get-a-room, and make-a-show" concept first conceived by neon artist Jeff Johnson. Winning the admiration of his peers, Johnson insisted at the time that the Reno area lacked adequate ideal art galleries for displaying unique works of the region's independent artists.

Opening these positive pathways were visual artists Dianna Sion, Esther Dunaway, Ann O'Lear and Chad Sorg—joined by performance artist Tova Ramos. The founders' inspiration stemmed partly from the internationally famous annual Burning Man festival during the week leading up to and through Labor Day weekend. These festivities, unassociated with NadaDada, are in the 1,000-square-mile Black Rock Desert 100 miles north of Reno.

The NadaDada founders also envisioned this idea as an alternative to the corporate-sponsored annual July Artown festival. Rather than hinge their concept on competition or juries that hand out awards, to their credit those who formed NadaDada also wanted a diverse process where all artists could participate regardless of medium or discipline.

For their first gathering in 2007 the organizers launched what at the time they first called the "Nada Motel" or "NadaDada Motel" which subsequently went simply by "NadaDada." According to published accounts, the founders derived the "NadaDada" term from "Dadaism," an anti-bourgeois art movement that swelled in Switzerland, Berlin and New York during the World War I era of the early 20th Century.

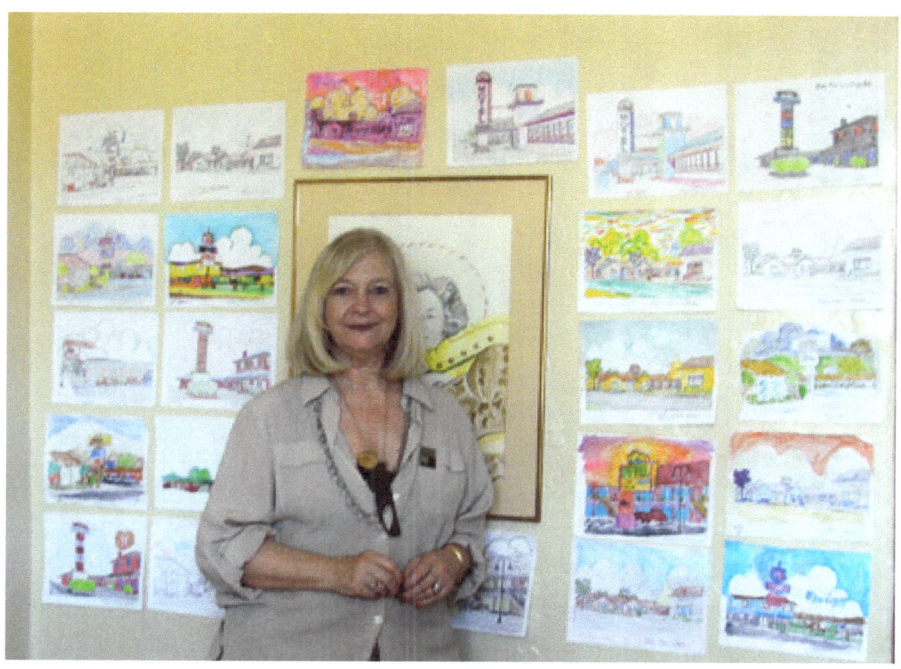

My room at the El Cortez Hotel in 2009

Professional and personal commitments prevented me from participating in NadaDada's inaugural festivities in 2007. I joined NadaDada in 2008.

Artists gathered at the El Cortez Hotel on West Second Street in downtown Reno, eventually expanding across South Arlington Avenue to the Town House Motor Lodge—the facility my late grandparents had once managed.

Within NadaDada's first two years the eclectic event became so popular that Patricia Leigh Brown wrote a full-page article in June 2009 in the "New York Times" that said: "Venice has its Biennale Basel, Switzerland has its Art Basel. And Reno has the NadaDada Motel, a jubilantly unpretentious art event in which some 100 artists rent rooms at two of the city's vintage hotels and motels and temporarily transform nicotine-infused rooms into art."

Energized and inspired by NadaDada as a lifelong artist, I have participated in the annual event since 2008. Right away my heart and my artistic spirit motivated me each year at NadaDada to create and display pen and ink drawings that eventually became the groundwork for this publication.

Since its inaugural years, NadaDada has moved from the El Cortez to a variety of Reno-area motels. One of the event's most popular venues remains Pat Campbell's Wildflower Village, added in 2011.

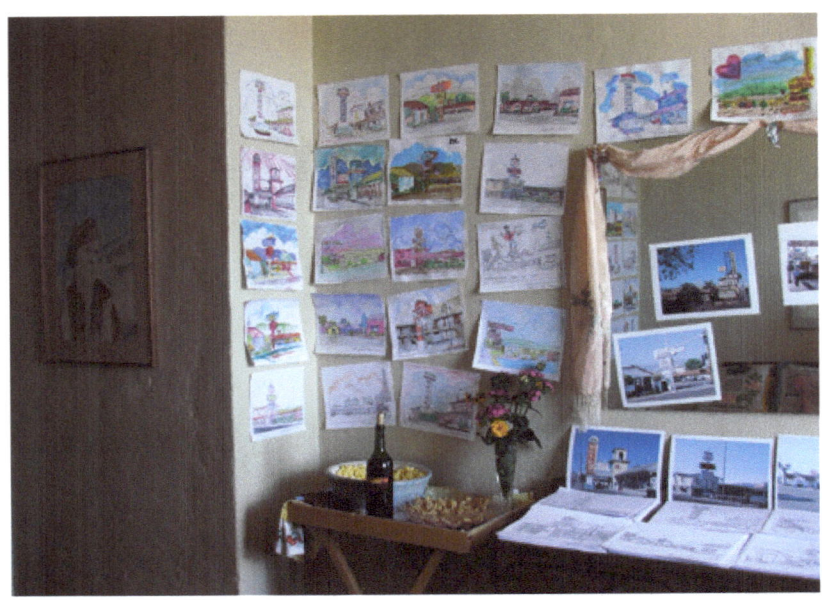
My room at the El Cortez Hotel in 2009

During my first year at NadaDada, streams of everyday, regular people enjoying the dozens of individual NadaDada artist rooms visited my room at the El Cortez. Many of these people sat at small tables in the room as they enjoyed coloring printouts that I provided of the initial motel illustrations.

As these participants left I hung their creations for display on the room's walls, visible to all subsequent visitors. Almost everyone spoke of the interesting, sharp diversity of the distinct and differing ways that people choose to color.

That initial display became so popular among NadaDada artists and visitors that I presented similar annual NadaDada coloring-book style displays—each time creating a new set of motels.

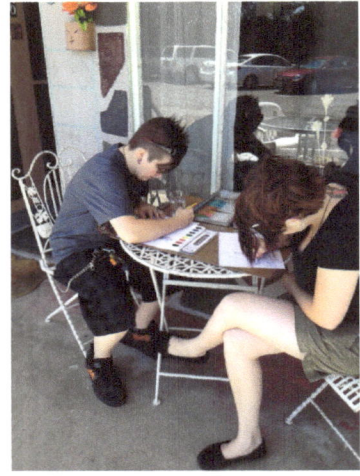
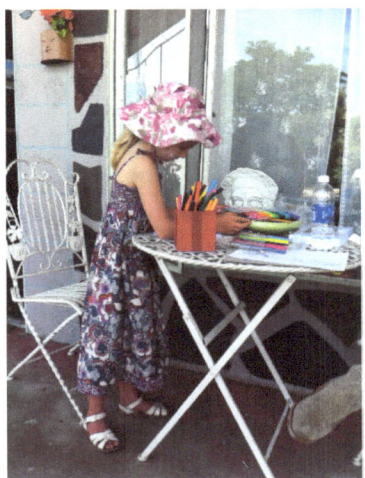
Participants coloring outside my studio at Wildflower Village

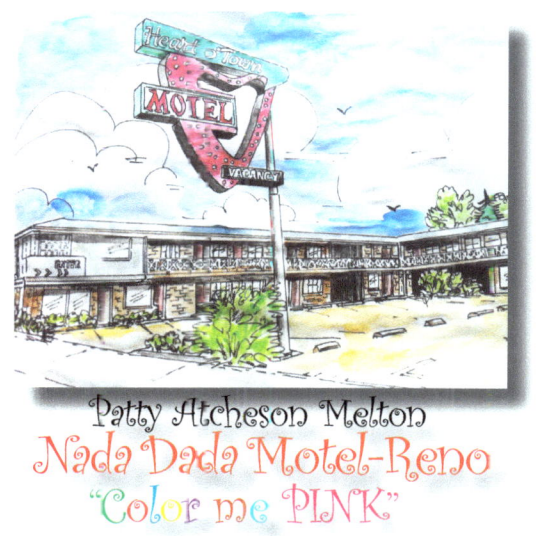

Patty Atcheson Melton
Nada Dada Motel-Reno
"Color me PINK"
June 16-19 2011

Everything within my personal universe commanded that I do this to the best of my ability. You see, as a society we're steadily losing a vital part of our vibrant history—the destruction and demolition of the classic old motels. Naturally, I let my heart guide me to many of the facilities that remained standing.

In fact, at the time that I generated images of the motels seen here among these pages, some facilities were surrounded by chain-link fences as the buildings awaited destruction via wrecking balls. This mirrored lyrics from the hit 1970 Joni Mitchell Tune, "Big Yellow Taxi," which proclaims "they paved paradise to put up a parking lot."

Several motels featured within these pages also remain standing, primarily along East Fourth Street and West Fourth Street in Reno—a roadway that had comprised the old U.S. Highway 40, a popular two-lane trans-America highway through the 1950s. Now primarily residences for low-income families. Those still standing once served to primarily entice weary motorists to temporarily stay in the Truckee Meadows. These visitors became a mid-twentith century mainstay to the local economy.

This publication emerged as a natural progression in my maturation process as both an artist and as a lover of history as well. The fact that my husband, Wayne, and I own a publishing company led me to fulfill the requests of many people who have asked me "I hope you make these prints into a coloring book."

Needless to say, I felt happy to oblige.

43

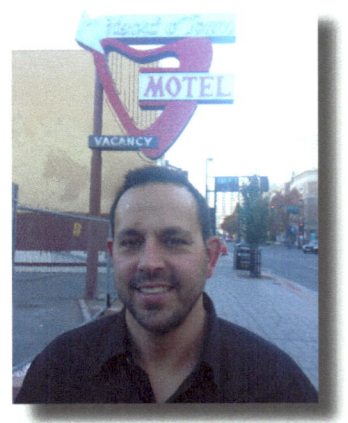

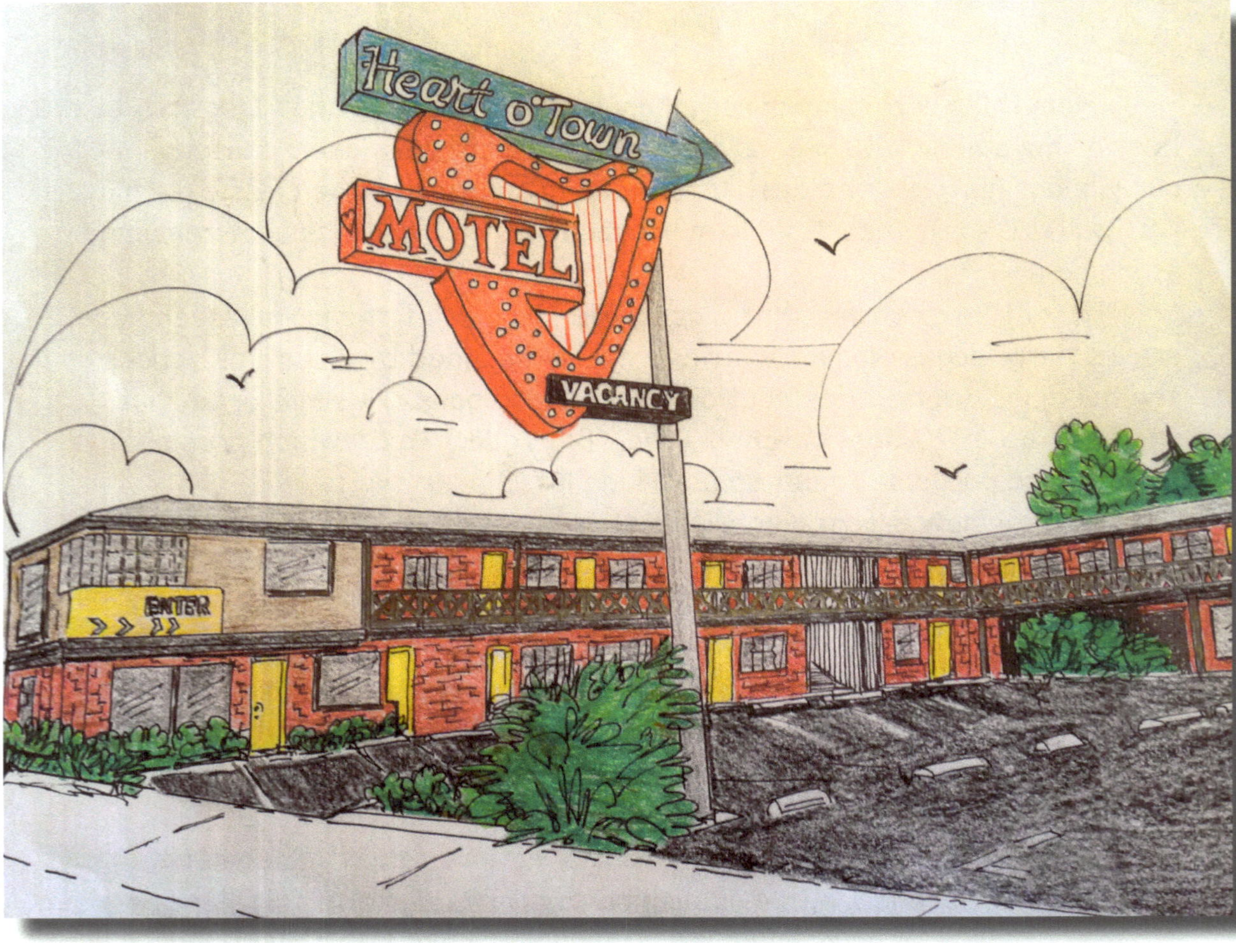

Will's coloring of the Heart o' Town Motel

The Magic of Neon Signs
Will Durham

The magic of neon signs wasn't invented in Nevada. Instead, it was perfected and elevated to a fine art here in the Silver State. Few places on earth could ever compete with the light shows put on every night on Fremont Street under the perpetual grin of Vegas Vic or on Virginia Street leading up to the world-famous Reno arch. The energy created in this concentrated space was similar to Times Square but in Nevada the properties exuded a unique character unparalleled in any city in the world. In Nevada it was the characters and legends, real or imagined, that gave our state a unique persona. On Virginia and Fremont streets, each property was basically pedaling the same product, gambling, and they had very limited street frontage to hawk their unique take on one armed bandits and green felt jungles. Cowboys, Indians, showgirls and giant chunks of gold all dressed in colorful neon beckoned visitors to take a chance on Nevada's version of the American dream.

In Reno, Highway 40 was a glowing compliment to the action happening in the casino core. Although much less frenetic, the long strand of motels around the main drag connecting Reno and Sparks put on a dazzling show of their own. Again basically selling the same service-lodging-it was the playful signage that gave each motel its unique character. The gorgeous diving swimmer from the Zephyr Motel would certainly be a welcome sight in the days before widespread effective air conditioning in automobiles. If travelers wanted to stay in the thick of things they could look for the sparkling giant heart at the aptly named Heart o' Town Motel.

Superstitious gamblers would probably skip the upside down horseshoe fronting the motel west of town and probably roll toward the Lucky Motel even though the flickering neon often spells "ucky". The animated car wheels on the Sandman Motel sign encouraged travelers to slow theirs and spend a night or two of peaceful dreams at their lodge. Whatever travelers were looking for, a dazzling neon sign would guide their way to a lodge that was right for everybody- like the Everybody's Inn.

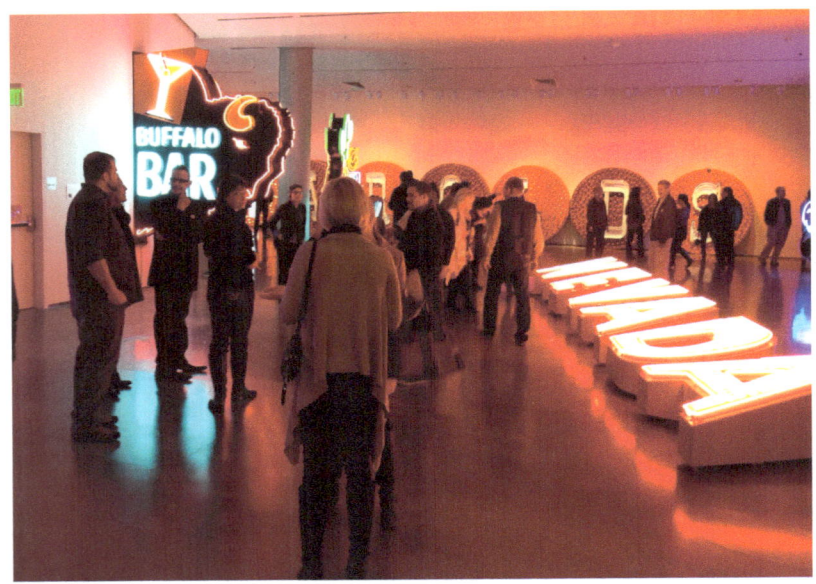

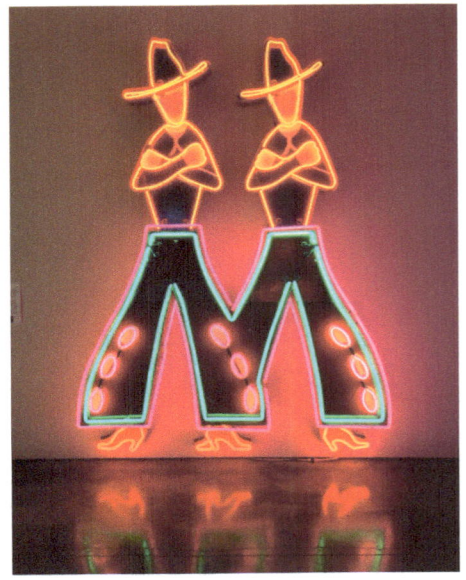

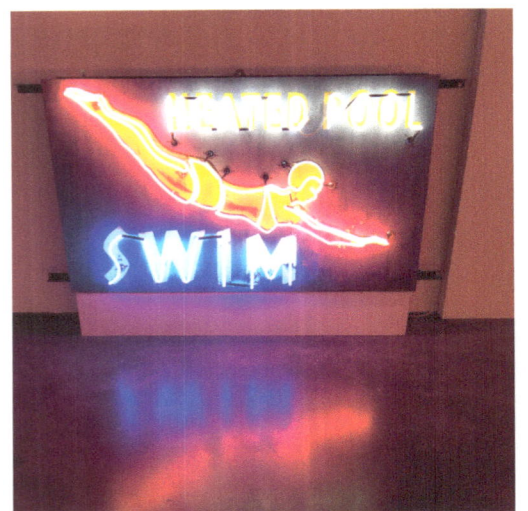

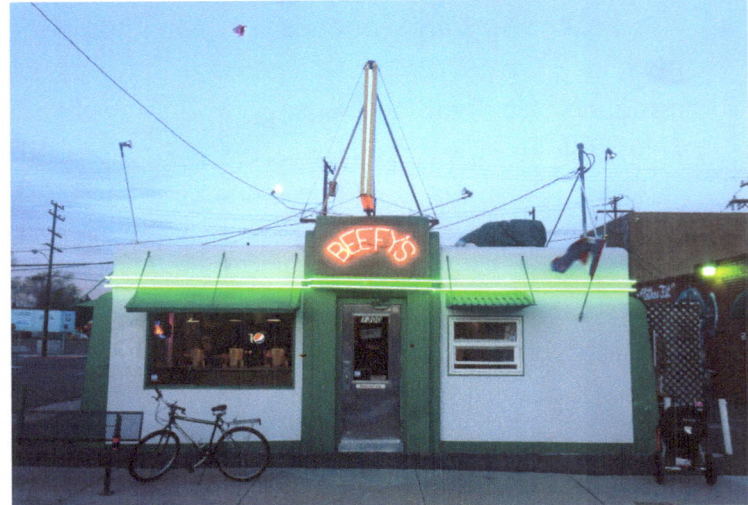

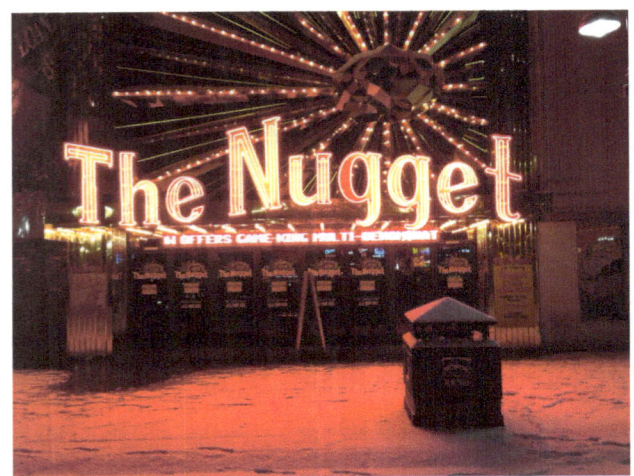

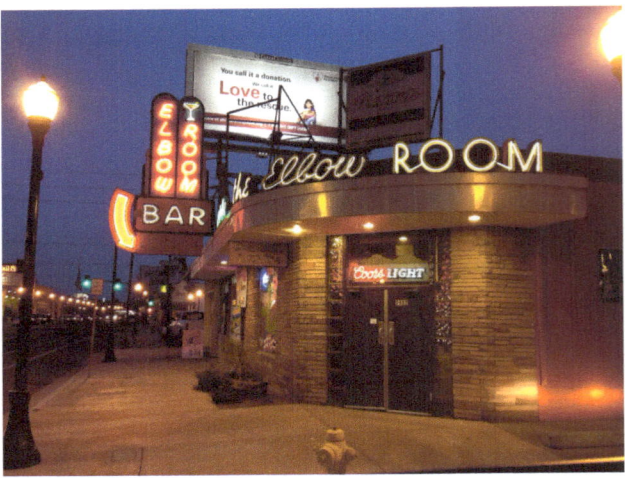

The modern era has forever changed the roadside culture of America and Nevada was certainly not immune to this unfortunate cultural shift. Interstates skirted main drags, chains and corporations squeezed out the mom and pops and inexpensively produced backlit plastic signs replaced the neon extravaganzas that personified the Silver State for a better part of the twentieth century. Motel demographics shifted from middle-class travelers to those that live on the fringe of society. All too often, these once-thriving lodges are overrun today with illicit activities. With very little need or incentive for owners to improve their properties, often the ghostly neon signs still stand proudly over their lodges to give enthusiasts a glimpse of what once was. In an attempt to combat perceived blight, many cities including Reno are requiring owners to remove these dark signs from dormant businesses.

Ever reinventing our image, Nevada has lost a great deal of the physical history that personified our state through much of the twentieth century. Despite the destruction of a lot of our historic structures, numerous groups and individuals have gone to great lengths to preserve the signs that gave these buildings their colorful character. In Las Vegas a group of preservationists with help from Young Electric Sign Company and The City of Las Vegas have been able to rescue some of the legendary signs from the Strip, Fremont Street and surrounding areas. Blockbusters from the Stardust and Moulin Rouge rest next to amazing motel signs from lodges like the Yucca, Normandie and La Concha. This project, the Neon Museum, has garnered attention from media outlets all over the world and frequently makes the lists of must-see attractions in Sin City.

The preservation efforts aren't always massive in scale. In Fallon 90 miles east of Reno, the Churchill Arts Council has recently relit the refurbished Lariat Motel sign. Now this animated neon cowboy will swing his lariat for a new generation to admire over his new location at Oak Park Art Center. At Wendover in extreme eastern Nevada, another neon cowboy avoided the scrap yard through the efforts of a community that wanted to hang on to a bit of our fascinating heritage. Wendover Will was moved from his perch at the Stateline casino and refurbished to welcome travelers to the gambling joints in West Wendover.

Please keep all this in mind when taking into account that when I was around eight years old I found myself fighting insomnia and feared the

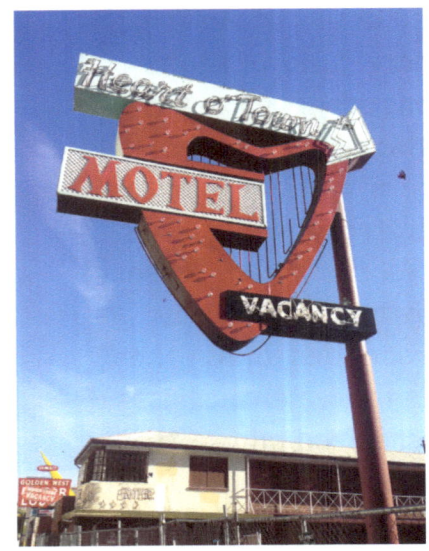
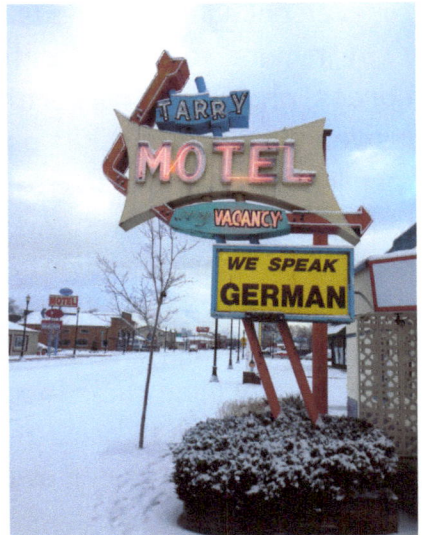
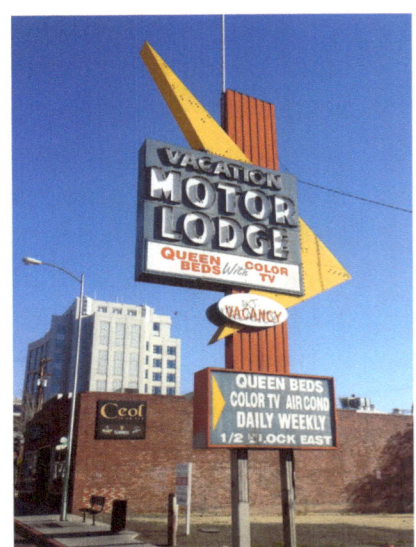
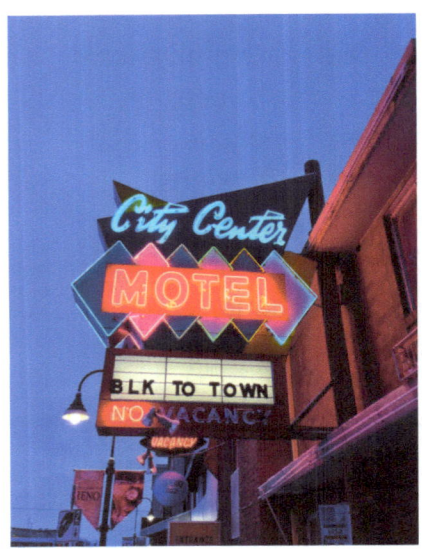
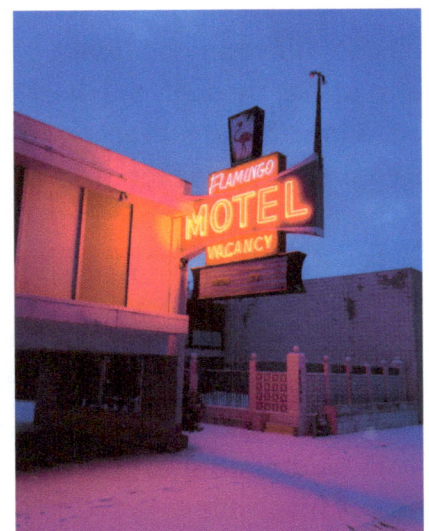
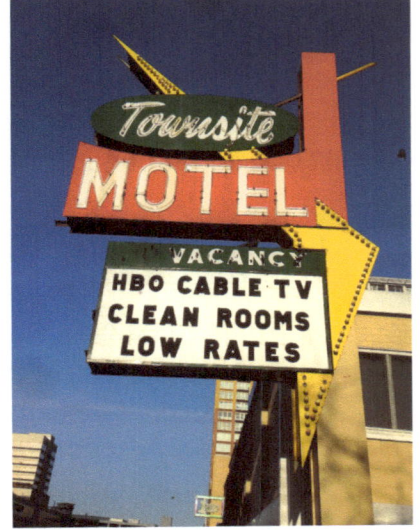
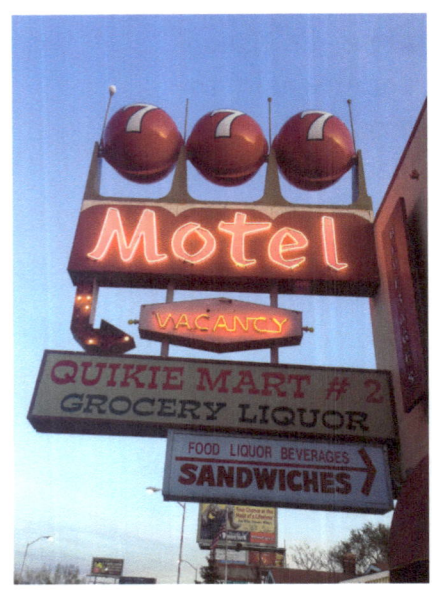
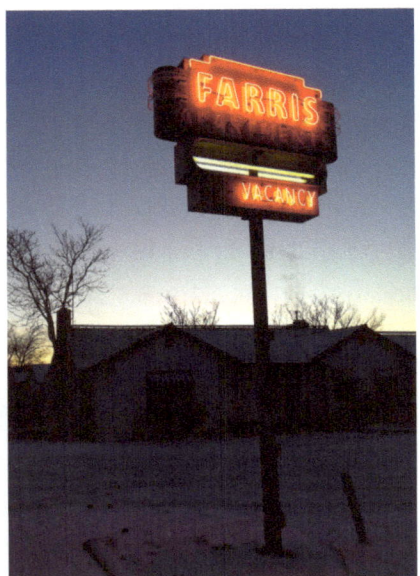
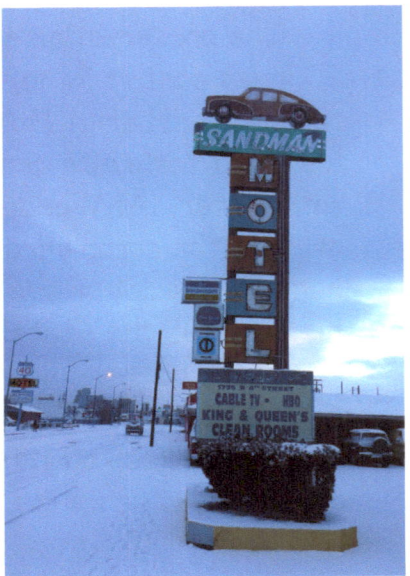

prospect of being the last person awake. If my immediate family fell asleep before I did, I would always look out my bedroom window to see the colorful glow from downtown Reno. I knew that as long as the neon was burning there was action and I wasn't the only one awake. I think this created a deep appreciation for the magic of neon signs.

In the '90s there was a wave of redevelopment that threatened not only the legendary casinos but also the 1940s and 1950s restaurants, bars and motels across the state. Around 1996 I preserved the signs from the Zephyr Motel on Old Highway 40. I didn't think this would be the start of a long-term preservation effort; it was just to decorate my lounge. In the months and years that followed I kept reading about the closures of some of the real legends of the gaming industry. I expected that there would be some benevolent hand that would swoop in and preserve these state treasures. I had a hard time thinking that these one-time giants would disappear as if they never existed. Without a lot or resources to devote to their preservation, I saved what I could in the form of signage. There were many days when I would ask myself why these signs were important and "was this worth the effort?" In the last 17 years I have been able to preserve signs from properties such as: Harolds Club, Nevada Club, The Mapes, Merry Wink Motel, Buffalo Bar and the Sahara Las Vegas.

In 2012, a portion of the preserved signs were shown at the Nevada Museum of Art in the **Light Circus-Art of Nevada Neon** show. It was great to see a glimpse of the magic that used to take place everyday on streets all over our state. It has always been my vision to create a permanent neon museum here in Reno. The signs that are in the Light Circus collection would create an attraction dazzling Nevada residents while luring tourists back to the Truckee Meadows, everyone motivated to see something with true character. With a little luck we will be able to bring these Nevada icons together and turn the lights back on.

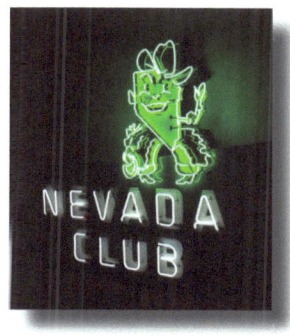

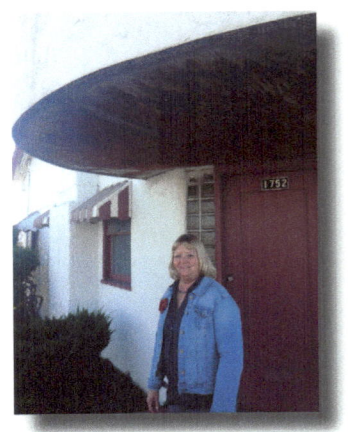

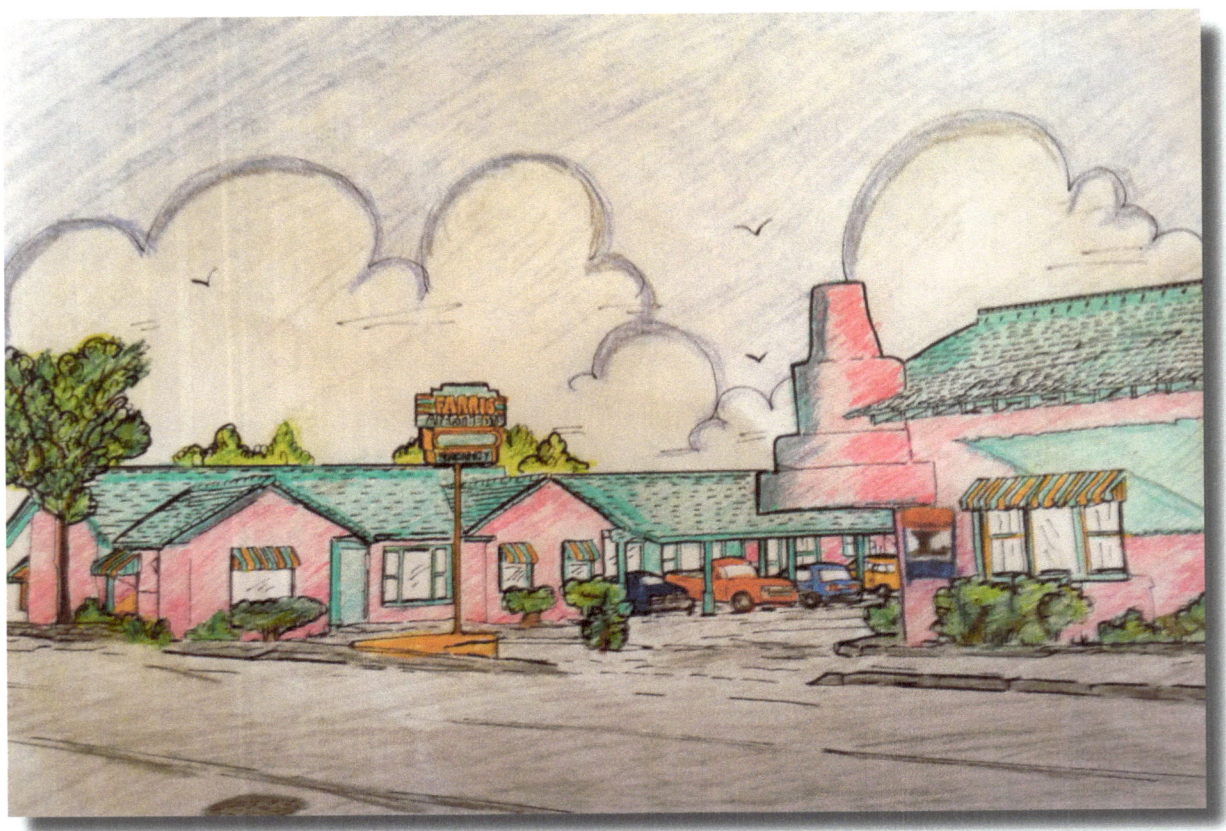

Cindy's coloring of the Farris Apartments

Cindy Ainsworth

Reno has been Cindy's home since 1978 when she moved here from Southern California to be with her husband Tom. Thinking they would only stay in Reno a few years, both fell in love with the quirky, unique city and Nevada's beautiful blue "big sky." Reno's diverse history caught Cindy's attention right away. Her historic interests include the various transportation developments associated with the Truckee Meadows like the Transcontinental Railroad, airmail routes and the Lincoln Highway.

Cindy is one of the founding members and a past president and board member of the Historic Reno Preservation Society (HRPS) and now holds the organization's part-time position of Administrator. She served on many HRPS committees and has researched, developed and organized historic walking and bus tours of the East Fourth Street Corridor. Currently, she is a member of the selection committee for HRPS' Neighborhood Preservation Fund which offers matching grants to homeowners and business owners so they may make improvements to their older properties. In 2007, HRPS celebrated its 10-year anniversary and is one of the longest surviving non-profit preservation organizations still operating in Reno.

The City of Reno Historical Resources Commission awarded Cindy the 2003 Distinguished Service Award for her work with HRPS and the community. In 2005, she was appointed by the Nevada State Historic Preservation Office to the Commission as a citizen representative and served as that panel's chair for two years. She has been involved in many city preservation issues including serving on the Reno Preservation Plan and Conservation District organizing committee and currently the RTC Fourth Street/Prater Way History Project committee. The Preservation Plan and the Powning Conservation District became a reality in 2008, a first for Reno.

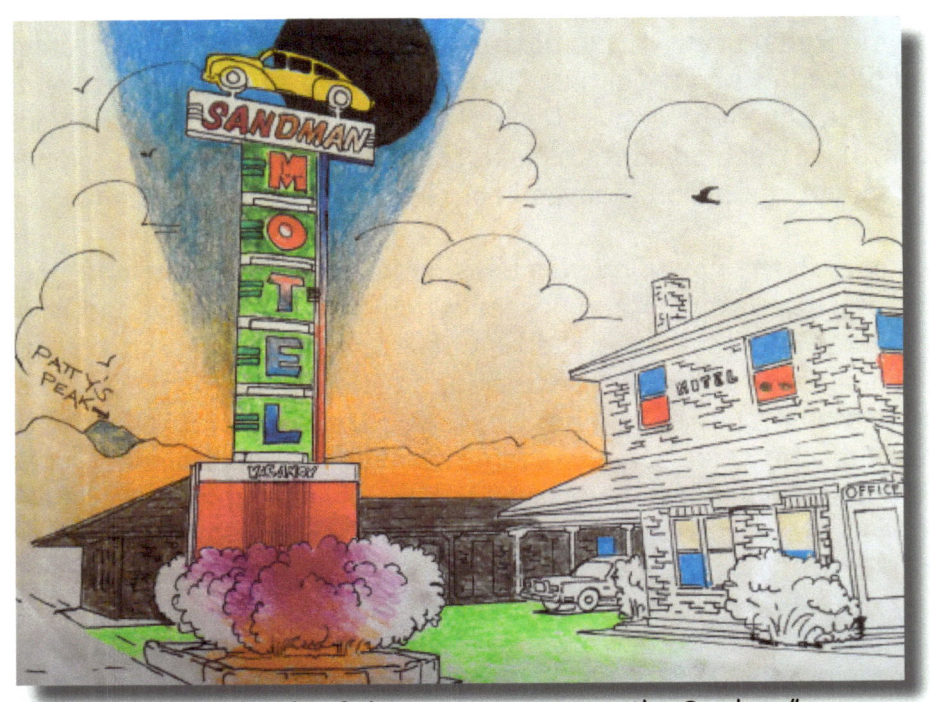

'The dark side of the moon passes over the Sandman"

-Jim McCormick '09

Dedication

To a great mentor, Jim McCormick, a longtime UNR art department faculty member and highly respected artist. I also dedicate this book to my family and especially to the memory of my grandparents, Oscar and Geneva Hedman for giving me fond memories of my motel days.

Acknowledgements

I would be remiss without giving a resounding note of thanks to Sharon Honig-Bear and Cindy Ainsworth for their boundless encouragement and support in getting this book printed.

Thank you again to Cindy for writing the foreward for this book. We are all blessed by her understanding, knowledge and commitment to Reno's history.

A virtual boxful of "thank-you" notices also must be proclaimed to the many NadaDada visitors and participants who colored my various annual pen-and-ink prints that eventually became the backbone for this book.

Additionally, added kudos and my eternal gratitude go out to the legendary neon collector Will Durham for participating in this project—a man instrumental in playing a vital, urgent role in serving as an inspiration and guide in the Reno area's historic preservation movement.

With equal importance, I would like to thank Wildflower Village owner Pat Campbell for her boundless and unwavering friendship and dedication to my art and also for her steadfast commitment to our community.

I want to thank the Historic Reno Preservation Society (HRPS) for their dedication to preserving and promoting historic resources for this community. I am proud to be a member and I will be donating 20 percent of the proceeds after taxes and costs from the sale of this book to HRPS.

Contact

Patty Atcheson Melton
pattymelton.com
create@pattymelton.com